GIFT OF
James Augustine Healy

Theatre in Ireland

Drama and Theatre Studies

ADVISORY EDITOR: HUGH HUNT
GENERAL EDITOR: KENNETH RICHARDS

Also in this series:

British Theatre, 1950–70
ARNOLD HINCHLIFFE

Theatre in the Age of Garrick
CECIL PRICE

The Theatre of Goethe and Schiller
JOHN PRUDHOE

A Short History of Scene Design in Great Britain
SYBIL ROSENFELD

Theatre in Ireland

MICHEÁL Ó hAODHA

ROWMAN AND LITTLEFIELD
Totowa, New Jersey

First published in the United States 1974
by Rowman and Littlefield, Totowa, N.J.

© Basil Blackwell 1974

All Rights Reserved. No part of this publication may be reproduced, stored in a retrieval system, or transmitted, in any form or by any means, electronic, mechanical, photocopying, recording or otherwise, without the prior permission of Basil Blackwell & Mott Limited.

LIBRARY OF CONGRESS CATALOGING IN PUBLICATION DATA

Ó hAodha, Micheál.
  Theatre in Ireland.

  (Drama and theatre studies)
  Bibliography: p.
  1. English drama—Irish authors—History and criticism.
2. Theater—Ireland. I. Title.
PR8789.O4 822'.009 73-21838
ISBN 0-87471-499-0

Printed in Great Britain by
Alden and Mowbray Ltd at the Alden Press, Oxford
and bound at the Kemp Hall Bindery

Contents

List of Plates	vii
Acknowledgments	ix
Introduction	xi
Chapter 1. A Broken Tradition	1
Chapter 2. The Nineteenth Century and Boucicault	12
Chapter 3. The Founders of the National Theatre	22
Chapter 4. Synge and the Abbey Play	40
Chapter 5. Synge's Successors	60
Chapter 6. The Abbey Style and its Influence	77
Chapter 7. Poetry on the Fringe	92
Chapter 8. O'Casey and After	105
Chapter 9. The Gate Theatre and Some Actors	119
Chapter 10. The End of the Beginning	131
Chapter 11. Rebels without Riots	141
Bibliography	157

List of Plates

(*Between pp 130 and 131*)

1. *The Plough and the Stars*, Abbey Theatre production
2. *Look at the Heffernans!* by Brinsley Macnamara, Abbey Theatre production
3. *The Well of the Saints* by J.M. Synge. Abbey Theatre production, 1970
4. *Borstal Boy* by Brendan Behan. Abbey Theatre production, 1967
5. *The Shaughraun* by Dion Boucicault. Abbey Theatre production, 1967
6. Lady Gregory by Gerald Festus Kelly
7. William Butler Yeats by Sean O'Sullivan
8. J.M. Synge by J.B. Yeats
9. Frank Fay by J.B. Yeats
10. William G. Fay by J.B. Yeats
11. F.J. McCormick by Sean O'Sullivan
12. Sara Allgood by Sarah Purser
13. Maire O'Neill by J.B. Yeats

LIST OF PLATES

14. Michael MacLiammoir
15. Hilton Edwards
16. The Old Abbey Theatre, 1904–51
17. The New Abbey Theatre, 1966
18. Interior of the old Abbey Theatre, from the balcony

Acknowledgments

I have to thank the following for permission to include various quotations: the Talbot Press, Limited, Dublin for those from *The Stage Irishman* by G. C. Duggan, and *The Story of Ireland's National Theatre* by Dawson Byrne; the Clarendon Press, Oxford for extracts from *The Early Irish Stage* by William S. Clark; Irish University Press and Dr. E. MacLysaght for those from *Irish Life in the Seventeenth Century*; Routledge & Kegan Paul and Gabriel Fallon for a passage from *Sean O'Casey: The Man I Knew* and the same publishers and Alan Simpson for that from *Beckett and Behan*; the Cultural Relations Committee of the Department of Foreign Affairs, Dublin for extracts from Micheál MacLiammóir's booklet *Theatre in Ireland*; Rupert Hart-Davis for a passage from *The Scenic Art* by Henry James; A. D. Peters and Macmillan & Company for an extract from *My Father's Son* by Frank O'Connor; A. P. Watt, Senator Michael Yeats and Macmillan & Company for extracts from *The Collected Works of W. B. Yeats*; and the Mercier Press, Cork, for passages from *Synge and Anglo-Irish Literature* by Daniel Corkery. I wish to thank my fellow Directors of the Abbey Theatre for the illustrations included in a work for which they are otherwise not responsible.

Introduction

It is one of the paradoxes of Irish history that the Irish, with their flair for the dramatic in public and in private, have no tradition of theatre in the historic sense. For over three centuries, Ireland has been a hotbed for actors, most of whom, for the greater part of their lives, adorned every country's capital but their own. Many playwrights of Irish birth from Ludowick Barry who wrote in Shakespeare's day to Samuel Beckett, the most widely known dramatist of the Space Age, have a place in the annals of drama. One need only mention the writers of comedy alone—George Farquhar, Oliver Goldsmith, Richard Brinsley Sheridan, Oscar Wilde, Bernard Shaw—to realize the measure of their contribution to world drama.

But we should not conclude that such achievements are widely accepted, even by the well-informed, as proof of Ireland's contribution to the drama. On the contrary, these are some of the big names in the most authoritative books on English drama and the British theatre. Even those writers who were romantically and popularly accepted as Irish, such as Dion Boucicault, are often relegated to the tributary streams of regional and dialect playwriting and are only regarded as important in so far as they helped to swell the main current of English dramatic endeavour.

There are, of course, historic reasons for such anomalies. Although Ireland has a literature in Irish stretching back for

INTRODUCTION

almost fifteen centuries to the Early Christian period, no dramatic work in the language appeared until the end of the last century. The old literature contains fragmentary passages in dialogue and contains an abundance of material for drama in prose and verse. Moreover, this work was part of a centuries-old oral tradition. Like much of great imaginative literature, the Gaelic epics and sagas were conceived as something to be spoken. The shanachie or storyteller had a keen sense of the dramatic but it was by the fireside, not on a stage, that he perfected his craft. It may well be that he favoured a solo performance, a one-man show, preferring to do all the talking himself rather than to share the dialogue with others. It is certain that the native population had little or no part in the miracle and morality plays which were staged in Dublin and other towns in medieval times. During the great flowering of Elizabethan drama, the Irish were fighting for their lives outside the Pale. After the first theatre was opened in Dublin in 1637, theatre remained for nearly two centuries within the control of a resident ruling class. Drama, therefore, spread no roots outside the Pale and the larger towns. Despite a flourishing amateur movement, Irish theatre has remained largely a Dublin growth to this day.

Although it was a useful label in the past, the term 'Anglo-Irish' has become somewhat meaningless as applied to drama in English written by Irishmen. Many playwrights of Irish birth have made a considerable contribution to the English Theatre both before and after the rise of a native dramatic movement at the end of the last century. Colonialism, whatever virtues it may have in other respects, had not been very fruitful in the dramatic field. It is true that a tentative Irishness can be discerned in the work of Sheridan, Goldsmith and others. But it was only after the advent of the Abbey Theatre that an indigenous Irish drama developed. This is manifest in the emergence of the one distinctive strain which Ireland has contributed to world drama, the folk or peasant play.

The Irish note is so dominant in the later drama that it is more rewarding to pose the question nowadays 'Is it a good

INTRODUCTION

play?' rather than 'Is it an Irish play?' It is more or less indisputable that there exists in Ireland a corpus of drama written in English which was certainly not part of the English theatre. In the eighteenth and nineteenth centuries, most of this work was associated with the reign of the Ascendancy and might with some justification be called colonial drama. To some critics, such as Professor Daniel Corkery, this is enough to condemn it out of hand—but unjustly so. The Ascendancy, for all their faults which do not require chronicling here, made a definite contribution to the social and cultural life of Dublin and the larger towns. The evolution of political events ended their dominance except in the north-east of the country which remained under British rule. But in Belfast, groups such as the Ulster Literary Theatre strove to develop a regional theatre on the lines of the Abbey.

The rise of a native drama, as exemplified by the Abbey Theatre, must be measured not only against the colonial theatre of earlier centuries but in relation to such diverse ventures as the Theatre of Ireland, the Ulster Literary Theatre, Edward Martyn's Irish Theatre, the Drama League, the Gate Theatre and the amateur movement. For over half a century, an intermittent controversy has raged between the advocates of an international theatre and the upholders of an indigenous drama movement. The advocates of a native drama, as exemplified in the National Theatre, have been guilty, at times, of a certain insularity and chauvinism in their efforts to nurture a distinctively Irish theatre. Their main justification is the work of playwrights such as Synge and O'Casey whose best work although written for the National Theatre transcends nationalism and is of international importance.

Nowadays, the idea is gaining ground that the Irish theatre has become embedded in the rut of tradition. It is felt that Irish theatre must be subjected to the winds that blow across the sea from Europe and that audiences must benefit from such exposure. This good and praiseworthy aim has given life and vitality to the Abbey's experimental annexe, the Peacock Theatre. The future of the Irish theatre may well rest in the development of the Peacock's rôle as a theatre workshop where young actors, young playwrights and young audiences can shape the drama of tomorrow.

It is manifestly easier to break with tradition than to create a tradition. Too often, in the past, the results of experimentation and theatrical novelty have proved sterile as far as original creative writing is concerned. One can easily detect the second-hand and derivative work which stems from a too close reproduction of the model provided by Broadway and international successes. In rejecting what it considers provincialism, this school of thought, on occasions, has succumbed to the worst provincialism of all, the aping of what is new or novel elsewhere in a totally uncritical fashion.

The ideas of James Joyce and the plays of Samuel Beckett may well be a portent of the arrival of a supranational phase in the Irish theatre. Neither of these writers adhered to the Yeatsian ideal of a national drama. Joyce, like Edward Martyn, was a fervid Ibsenite and from his youth had rejected the ideas of Yeats and Frank Fay. What they have in common with a long line of playwrights of Irish birth, since Farquhar's day, is a feeling for language. Techniques have changed, styles of presentation have been revolutionised, but the constant factor is a gift for dialogue and a delight in the sparkle and iridescence of the spoken word.

CHAPTER ONE

A Broken Tradition

It was a Scot, John Ogilby, a Master of the Revels under the Lord Deputy, Thomas Wentworth, Earl of Strafford who built the first theatre in Ireland, in Werburgh Street, Dublin, in 1637. Although it survived until 1641, when the Puritans came to power, the most notable production at Werburgh Street was by the late Elizabethan playwright, James Shirley. At Ogilby's request, he came to Dublin as resident playwright at the Werburgh Street Theatre and staged, in 1640, the first historical play on an Irish subject, *St. Patrick for Ireland*.

The Irishman had made an occasional appearance on the English stage since Shakespeare's day. Allusions to Ireland, however, were indirect and curious when not contemptuous or slight. Phrases in the Irish language were incorporated in the dialogue of the anonymous *Famous History of Thomas Stukeley* which was printed in London in 1605. It was probably written by someone with first-hand knowledge of Elizabethan Ireland. Saint Patrick's appearance on a Dublin stage, in 1640, was something of a portent, not because he was the national saint but because he was portrayed by an English Catholic dramatist to a largely Protestant Dublin audience. It was no easy task, as Shirley recalled:

> I'll tell you what a poet says: two year
> He has lived in Dublin, yet he knows not where
> To find the city . . .

A BROKEN TRADITION

> When he did live in England, he heard say
> That here were men loved wit and a good play;
> That here were gentlemen and lords; a few
> Were bold to say there were some ladies too;
> This he believed, and though they are not found
> Above, who knows what may be underground?

A great deal, in fact, was underground. The miracle plays which had been produced in an earlier period had been succeeded by dramatic entertainments staged by the trade guilds. These were chiefly pageants and more likely to feature Saint George than Saint Patrick although he was already a folk-hero of native Irish literature. Dramatic dialogues between the pagan Oisín and the Christian saint had long been popular among the native Irish and these apocryphal disputations might have been the starting-point of a school of Irish drama. Before Shirley's visit, Dublin had seen nothing of how the medieval drama had developed in Elizabethan and Jacobean eras. But an up-dated miracle play written by a Catholic for a largely Protestant audience in seventeenth-century Ireland could not hope to succeed. Saint Patrick, through no fault of Shirley, emerges as the first stage Irishman, a rôle which he still fills on the National Holiday, particularly in the United States. A few years ago, the archetypal figure of the mitred saint driving the snakes out of Ireland suffered a jolt when some negroes in South Chicago paraded a black Saint Patrick in opposition to the traditional Saint Patrick's Day Parade and all the shenanigans that accompany it. Irish scholars, unwittingly, have added to the confusion by their insistence that there were two or perhaps three Saint Patricks of different origins. The stage Irishman, the Paddy of the Saint Patrick's Day variety, has become as ubiquitous as his eponymous prototype.

At least one Irish-born writer, Henry Burnell of Castleknock, near Dublin, contributed plays to the Werburgh Street repertoire. On St. Patrick's Day, 1639, his tragi-comedy, *Langdartha*, introduced some local colour in the person of 'a humorous gentlewoman dressed in an Irish gown tucked-up to mid-leg, with a broad basket-hilt sword on, hanging on a great belt, brogues on her feet, her hair dishevelled, and a pair of long neck'd big rowll'd spurs on her heels'.[1]

After the Restoration John Ogilby returned to Dublin and in 1662 opened the Smock Alley Theatre. This theatre, like Werburgh Street, was the special preserve of a resident ruling class who took their standards and their plays from London. The resident companies were imported from England and few native-born actors appeared on the bills. One of the first Irish actors to rise to eminence in his native city was Robert Wilks who in 1691 played the lead in *Othello* at the Smock Alley Theatre. He began life as a government official but used to frequent Smock Alley backstage and read cue speeches for the actors at rehearsals. The Williamite Wars had closed the theatre and Wilks's opportunities at first were confined to amateur and private performances. His Othello, under Ashbury's management, was the beginning of one of the most brilliant theatrical careers of that generation. In 1693, Wilks moved to Drury Lane, London, but he was tempted back by an offer from Ashbury of the exorbitant salary of sixty pounds per annum plus a 'benefit'. According to a theatre critic of the time, he proved to be worth the money: 'Mr. Wilks' excellence in comedy was never once disputed. . . . He was not only perfect in every part he acted, but in those that were concerned with him in every scene, which often prevented mistakes.' As a result of gossip which retailed an affair between Wilks and Mrs. Ashbury, the manager's wife, Wilks left again for Drury Lane in 1699 but only after Mrs. Ashbury, in order to pacify her husband, 'had delivered a sworn statement to the rector of Saint Michan's before the Communion table'. For over thirty years, Wilks held his place in the first rank of actors on the London stage. After his death in 1732, Doctor Johnson wrote of him as deserving 'to be remembered for his virtues, which are not often found in the world, and perhaps less often in his profession than in others'.

The morals of the Dublin theatre were no better than any-

[1] William Smith Clark, *The Early Irish Stage*, 1955, p. 38.

where else in Restoration days. John Dunton thought Smock Alley 'no unfit name for a place where such great opportunities are given for the making of lewd bargains'.[2] In the upper gallery there were small boxes over the stage where fashionable men-about-town and students from Trinity College could entertain a paramour with discretion. As the prologue to the comedy *St. Stephen's Green* has it, the Dublin gallants

> Strut in the pit, survey the Gallery
> In hopes to be lur'd up by some kind She[3]

One of the Trinity College playgoers in the 1690s was George Farquhar. His father is said to have been a clergyman in Derry but he did not inherit much respect for the cloth and was expelled from Trinity College for an irreverent jest in a scriptural test. Through the influence of Robert Wilks, he obtained an engagement as an actor in Smock Alley where he acquitted himself creditably in minor rôles. While playing in Dryden's *The Indian Emperor* he forgot to change his sword for a foil, and wounded a fellow-actor so badly that Farquhar decided never to act again. He next took to a more earnest form of sword-play by joining the Earl of Orrery's regiment as a lieutenant. *Love and a Bottle* and *The Constant Couple* proved so successful that he was induced to leave the army and devote himself exclusively to drama. He never offered to Ireland the first fruits of his labours and so London, once more, gained what Dublin lost. He only returned to Dublin once, in 1704, when he appeared as Sir Harry Wildair in his own comedy *The Constant Couple*. This benefit netted him one hundred pounds but according to a contemporary account he executed the rôle so loudly that his friends were ashamed for him. Ill health had begun to spoil his chances. But he did manage to write his best and last play *The Beaux' Stratagem* in six weeks on a sick-bed. He died in his twenty-ninth year while his last play was taking London by storm. Of Farquhar's achievement and early death, Leigh Hunt wrote:

[2] Edward MacLysaght, *Irish Life in the Seventeenth Century*, 1950, p. 238.
[3] John Dunton, *The Dublin Scuffle*, 1699, pp. 339-40.

He was becoming gayer and gayer when death, in the shape of a sore anxiety called him away, as if from a pleasant party, and left the house ringing with his jest.

Farquhar was the first dramatist to write easy flowing prose dialogue for comedy, the form later perfected by his compatriots Goldsmith and Sheridan. In the part of Sir Harry Wildair, he provided a suitable vehicle later for another famous Dubliner, Peg Woffington.

Dublin tradition has it that Peg Woffington as a child sold apples and oranges at theatre doors until she was 'discovered' by the famous French tight-rope dancer, Madame Violante, who ran a fashionable booth in Fownes Court. There she received her first training and made her first appearance in a song and dance act.

This daughter of a Dublin bricklayer and a washerwoman was born in 1720; she had her first great success at the age of sixteen at the Smock Alley Theatre as Ophelia in *Hamlet*. A few years later, she is said to have eloped with a young buck named Taaffe, the son of the Earl of Carlingford and a cousin of the illustrious Field-Marshal Taaffe of Austria. Taaffe, it seems, abandoned her in favour of a rich heiress.

Her romances with the great Garrick and, believe it or not, Doctor Johnson and Edmund Burke, have been the subject of several novels and plays. She was a witty woman and a thorn in the side of her fellow-actresses, Kitty Clive and the blue-eyed Bellamy, with whom she quarrelled outrageously. Whatever her temperament, her exceptional beauty is evident in the authentic portrait by Lewis, the scene painter at Smock Alley, now in the National Gallery, Dublin.

Her favourite rôle was Sir Harry Wildair, the wild reckless man about town, in Farquhar's *The Constant Couple*. But she had no failures during her dazzling career, in spite of a voice that her contemporaries describe as 'almost unmanageable in its harshness'.

In May 1757, while playing the part of Rosalind in *As You Like It*, she collapsed in a seizure and tottered feebly to what proved to be her last exit.

To the dismay of theatregoers and to the delight of moralists, she spent the last three years of her life in retirement at Teddington where she acted the part of Lady Bountiful to the poor and needy. Apart from the portrait in the National Gallery, nothing remains in Dublin to recall her triumphs, save that famous institution, Mercer's Hospital, for which she gave a benefit performance when she was only seventeen years of age.

Although Charles Shadwell, early in the eighteenth century, wrote several plays for Smock Alley with Irish settings and Irish characters and with a Dublin audience in mind, standards remained low and there is little specifically Irish in spirit. The mid-century, however, saw the heyday of that ubiquitous character, the stage Irishman. The phrase 'the wild Irish' had been current since the days of Giraldus Cambrensis and it is understandable that a colonial theatre should give to a colonial audience the kind of Irishman they expected. The larger towns, and Dublin in particular, were outposts of British rule. And wherever a theatre existed, at one time or other, since the seventeenth century, it was under alien patronage and control. The earliest stage presentations of Irishmen in drama were clearly drawn from life but it was the degeneration of stage writing itself that produced the stereotype of the stage Irishman. An early example of the type of boisterous knock-about who later became the typical stage Irishman is to be found in *The Brave Irishman* or *Captain O'Blunder* by another Smock Alley actor-manager, Thomas Sheridan.

The author, the father of the more famous Richard Brinsley, was of a County Cavan family. His father, the friend and biographer of Swift, died while his son was still a student in Trinity College. Although his most famous creation, Captain O'Blunder, may not have been intended as a gross caricature, he is the prototype of worse to come. O'Blunder is 'above six feet high, a great huge back and shoulders, with a great long sword which he calls his sweetlips—carries a great oaken cudgel which he calls his shillela—add to this a great pair of Jack-boots, a Cumberland pinch to his hat, an old red coat and a damn'd potatoe face'.[4] His speech abounds in Irish bulls and blunders that foreshadow Richard Brinsley's creations, Sir Lucius O'Trigger and Mrs. Malaprop in *The Rivals*. In the preface to this play, the younger Sheridan, Richard Brinsley, defends himself against any charge of travesty or of belittling his fellow-countrymen: 'If the condemnation of this comedy could have added one spark to the decaying flame of national attachment to the country supposed to be reflected on, I should have been happy in its fate, and might with truth have boasted that it had done more real service in its failure than the successful morality of a thousand stage-novels will ever effect'. None the less, in his farce *St. Patrick's Day or The Scheming Lieutenant*, the younger Sheridan in the character of Lieutenant O'Connor moves dangerously close to banality and blather.

The most distinguished Dublin actor in the eighteenth century was Spranger Barry, born in Skinner's Row, Dublin, in 1719, the son of a silversmith. After making his debut at Smock Alley in 1744, he moved to Covent Garden where, for a time, he rivalled David Garrick in the estimation of London theatregoers. Opinion on their respective merits was divided. 'With the audience,' wrote a contemporary critic, 'Garrick commanded most applause, but Barry elicited more tears.' Perhaps the best tribute to Barry's acting ability was that of a lady who had seen both Garrick and Barry play Romeo: 'Had I been Juliet to Garrick's Romeo, so impassioned was he that I should have expected him to come up to me in the balcony; but had I been Juliet to Barry's Romeo, so tender and seductive was he, I should certainly have jumped down to him.'

In 1754, Spranger Barry returned to Dublin, took a lease of a music-hall in Crow Street and acquired several lots of ground so that he could erect a stage as big as that of Drury Lane. This project cost him over £22,000 before the theatre was opened in October 1759. Under the patronage of the Duke of Dorset the theatre flourished for a time, but the strenuous opposition of the well-established playhouses in Smock Alley and Aungier Street involved him in considerable loss.

[4] G. C. Duggan, *The Stage Irishman*, 1937, p. 198.

For a time, it seemed that Mrs. Abington, an actress of star quality, would save the fortunes of Crow Street, but the defection of another leading actor, Henry Mossop, to Smock Alley involved Barry in further financial difficulties. He was a dedicated and imaginative actor-manager. Spranger Barry presented Richard Aldridge in the very first Irish ballet, *The Irish Lilt*, based on original Irish airs. Charles Coffey in his ballad-opera, *The Beggar's Wedding*, a thinly veiled satire on the Dublin Corporation in the style of Gay's *The Beggar's Opera*, introduced such well-known airs as 'Eileen Aroon' and 'Lillibulero'. But Barry's greatest asset, in the Crow Street venture, was another Irish actor-playwright, Charles Macklin.

Macklin, whose real name was MacLoughlin, was born in Derry in 1697. According to himself, six of his uncles took part in the siege of Derry, three in King James's army and three on the Williamite side. In his early youth, he was apprenticed to a saddler but ran away to Dublin where he worked as a pot-boy. He left for London, about 1725, where after a spell as a barman, he became a touring actor. Of quarrelsome temperament, he was convicted at the Old Bailey in 1735 for the manslaughter of a fellow-actor. This and his naturalistic approach to acting, in an age accustomed to the declamation and statuesque dignity of Quin and Booth, made him many enemies among his fellow-actors.

Macklin's performance in *The Merchant of Venice*, in which he portrayed Shylock not as a comic figure but as a serious and tragic character, earned him one of the most pithy and enduring critiques ever bestowed on an actor—

> This is the Jew
> That Shakespeare drew

—Pope's extempore couplet on Macklin's performance. But an anonymous critic was less flattering: 'In public his attention was engrossed with the importance of pauses. He had his *simple* pause, his *middle* pause, and his *grand* pause. The last was his favourite and he sometimes indulged so long in it, that the prompter, supposing he had forgotten his part, has often given him his cue, and by repeating the words still louder, made him quit the stage and complain of being interrupted.'[5]

The best of Macklin's plays is *The Man of the World* in which he excelled as Sir Pertinax MacSycophant. *The True Born Irishman or The Fine Irish Lady*, written in 1762, held the stage in Dublin for many years. This satiric piece concerns a Mrs. Diggerty, an Irish lady who, after a short visit to London despises everything Irish including her married name O'Dogherty. She suffers from 'the Irish Fine Lady's delirium or the London vertigo'—'the devil a thing in this poor country but gives her the spleen and the vapours'. She cultivates 'a new kind of English that's no more like our Irish English, than a coxcomb's fine gilded chariot is like a Glassmanogue noddy—she is no longer the plain, modest, good-natured domestic, obedient Irish O'Dogherty, but the travelled rampant, high lif'd prancing English Mrs. Diggerty'.[6] But this early attempt at social satire was a failure with London audiences. Goldsmith was wiser in his generation. Although the cast of his mind was un-English, he omitted Irish characters from his plays, preferring to draw on childhood memories of the Three Jolly Pigeons and the Irish midlands. Other Irish-born playwrights such as Hugh Kelly, Arthur Murphy and John O'Keeffe made a contribution to the eighteenth-century drama without displaying anything more than native wit and a tentative Irishness. It was left to an Irish actor, Robert Owenson or Mac Owen to introduce theatre audiences to the Irish language. In 1784, he staged benefits, at the Fishamble Street Theatre, which included songs in Irish which he sang with great effect. Here is an account of the opening night by his daughter, Lady Morgan: 'The first performance was to be altogether national, that is Irish, and *very* Irish it was. The play chosen was *The Carmelite* by Captain Jephson, with an interlude from Macklin's farce of *The Brave Irishman*, and a farce of O'Keeffe's *The Poor Soldier*. The overture consisted of Irish airs ending with the Volunteer's March which was chorused by the gallery to the accompani-

[5] *The Dramatic Inspector*, vol. 1, no. 9, Monday 22 July 1816, p. 202.
[6] Charles Macklin, *The True-Born Irishman*, 1783, Act I, p. 8.

ment of drums and fifes. . . . The National Theatre flourished. Everybody took boxes but few paid for them.'[7] This theatre closed in 1786. The Irish language, in a theatre context, was not to be heard of again for over a century. Theatre was to remain a foreign thing, a colonial creation, and the plays staged had little real connection with Irish life, and as a consequence had little influence or impact on the people as a whole. The best actors and playwrights had, of necessity, to leave Ireland for London or later for the United States. The fate of the provincial theatres in Belfast, Cork, Limerick and Galway was even more depressing. If Dublin was a sideshow of London, the theatres in the Irish provinces were reduced to the level of penny-gaffs.

In the late eighteenth century and well into the nineteenth century, amateur theatricals were staged in the shadow, if not within the walls, of the big houses of the Ascendancy. These gentlemen players, like gentlemen jockeys, kept aloof from the more robust conditions of the commercial arena. Patrons of the arts like the Earl of Charlemont, Luke Gardiner, Thomas Connolly of Castletown, the Earl of Kildare and the Countess of Ely ran private theatres where their friends and guests could display their talents in the elegant Georgian surroundings. The most famous was the Kilkenny Theatre where Thomas Moore met his beloved Betsy Dyke.

Occasionally, a professional player took part in these amateur theatricals, usually an actress in search of a titled husband or a touring actor down on his luck. One of the actresses who struck it lucky, matrimonially, was Mrs. Siddon's only rival, Elizabeth O'Neill. Like most of her contemporaries, she was born, as the saying goes, 'in the profession' at Drogheda in 1791 where her father was manager of a small fit-up company. While still a child she made her debut in Dublin as one of the Princes in the Tower in *Richard III*. But in 1812, a literary journal records that 'father and daughter were doing very ill in Dublin, half-starving while they waited for luck'. It happened that a popular actress, Mrs. Waldenstein, went on strike for higher pay and

[7] Peter Kavanagh, *The Irish Theatre* (1946), p. 284.

Elizabeth O'Neill took over, exciting 'such sensations of delight that the Irish capital was beside itself'. Dublin was not beside itself for long, as she left for Covent Garden where, in 1814, she appeared as Juliet, filling London with admiration and Mrs. Siddons with disgust. She had a short and brilliant career at Covent Garden where she starred in Shakespeare and many forgotten plays with Kemble and Macready. The end came suddenly in the play in which she began, *Richard III*, which seems to have been part of her destiny. She played Lady Anne to the Richard of Mr. Wrixon Becher of Kilfane, a member of Parliament for Mallow, at the Kilkenny Private Theatre. Her courtship ran more happily off the stage than on, for in 1819, she married Becher who soon afterwards was knighted.

For more than fifty years, Lady Becher lived as chatelaine of her husband's mansion at Ballygiblin, Co. Cork. She frequently held readings of Shakespeare but never referred to her professional career, not so much ashamed of the days of her glory as of her humble origin, an unpardonable offence in the eyes of Cork society in the years after the Union.

But it would be a mistake to underestimate the contribution of the resident ruling class to the social life of Irish cities, particularly in the last quarter of the eighteenth century. This small and largely alien aristocracy did much to maintain their own cultural standards. And from this class came the long line of Irish-born dramatists who greatly enriched the English theatre and made a positive contribution to world drama.

CHAPTER TWO

The Nineteenth Century and Boucicault

The first half of the nineteenth century is a black and dreary period in the annals of drama in Great Britain. It saw the emergence of closet-drama when poets wrote for the study, not for the stage, and when their impulse was more literary than dramatic. In this genre, a neglected Irish poet, George Darley, deserves mention as the first to recognise the dramatic possibilities of the life of Thomas à Becket; his unstaged verse play of that name gave a lead to Aubrey de Vere, Tennyson, T. S. Eliot and Jean Anouilh who have treated the subject since.

A more successful purveyor of verse drama was James Sheridan Knowles who, as his name indicates, was related to Richard Brinsley Sheridan and other notables of that family. Born in Cork, where his father was a schoolmaster, he was something of a child prodigy, having completed not only a play but an opera by the age of fourteen. In 1810, he joined Andrew Cherry's Company and played in Waterford with Edmund Kean who had not yet been hailed as the greatest tragedian of the age. It was at Kean's request that Knowles wrote his most successful tragedy *Virginius* in which Kean later appeared. William Charles Macready, the son of an Irish emigrant, had an earlier success in *Virginius* and in two other plays by Knowles, *Caius Gracchus* and *William Tell*. Between 1820 and 1835, Knowles established himself as a most prolific playwright and accomplished actor who is recalled affectionately in the reminiscences of Lamb and Hazlitt. After an illness, Knowles retired from the stage to become a Baptist preacher devoting his considerable talents to attacks on Catholics and the theatre.

Whenever old-timers of the theatre get together, the talk turns, sooner or later, to the melodramas of the last century, and someone is bound to mention, with an unmistakable affection and relish, *The Colleen Bawn*, *The Shaughraun* or *Arrah, na Pogue*. The plots and characters of these plays are known to many; the name of their author, Boucicault, is known to some, but only the flimsiest details of his life and career are known to most.

An air of mystery shrouds the playwright's birth and ancestry—a mystery which he himself encouraged. To add to the confusion he changed his name rather frequently; it appears, at different stages, as Dionysius Lardner Boursiquot, Dion Boursiquot, Lee Moreton, even Viscount Boucicault, until finally he settled for Dion Boucicault as 'a suitable patronymic to suggest the subtle magical qualities of a necromancer'. He was always ready to invest his own life with a share of the sensation and melodrama so characteristic of his plays. Once, in answer to the question 'Are you an Irishman?' he replied—a shade cryptically—'Sir, nature did me that honour'. And right enough, nature, colloquially speaking, seems to have done her share.

It is now generally accepted that he was the natural son of Dr. Dionysius Lardner, a lecturer, and editor of Lardner's Cabinet Cyclopedia, at whose residence, 47 Lower Gardiner Street, Dublin, he was born on St. Stephen's Day, 1820. His mother, Anne Darley Boursiquot, had separated in 1819 from her husband Samuel Boursiquot, a Dublin wine merchant of French descent. Dr. Lardner looked after his upbringing and he attended Dr. Geoghegan's Academy in Dublin and later at schools in Hampstead and Brentford.

His mother, Anne Darley Boursiquot, a sister of the poet George Darley, was connected by marriage with the Guinness family, and she secured a clerkship for her son at the St. James's Gate Brewery about 1839. He left this employment after a short time, and by the end of 1840 he had made his mark as a touring actor in England, under the name Lee Moreton. At Brighton, he played the leading rôle of Sir Giles Overeach in *A New Way to Pay Old Debts*. Soon after, he got his very first 'Irish' part in Samuel Lover's *Rory O'Moore*—the very first of the romantic melodramas which Dion was later to make famous.

During the next fifty years of his life, under the name Dion Boucicault, he became one of the best known actor-playwrights not only in Ireland and England but in America and Australia. His output was enormous; he is credited with one hundred and fifty plays most of which were adaptations from novels, like *The Collegians* by Gerald Griffin, his source for *The Colleen Bawn*, or from French plays and farces.

Boucicault inherited more than a name from the egregious Doctor Lardner, whom Thackeray satirised as 'Dionysius Diddler—spending all his money on clothes and in giving treats to the ladies of whom he was outrageously fond'. His son was equally lavish but more discreet. Between 1844 and 1848, he resided in Paris where he adopted the title Viscount Boucicault having married a wealthy Frenchwoman some years his senior. On his return to London, in deepest mourning, he explained to his friends that, while honeymooning in Switzerland, his wife had fallen down a precipice. When it later transpired that he was £1,000 the richer, under his wife's will, a mordant wit described it as 'his first adaptation from the French'.

His second wife, Agnes Robertson, an actress from Edinburgh, who survived him, played most of the feminine leads in his best-known plays and is said to have excelled in 'pathos of the simple old-fashioned ballad style'. When he was sixty-five years of age, Boucicault visited Australia and married Louise Thorndyke, another actress. Mrs. Robertson-Boucicault, to preserve her reputation, sued for a divorce but Boucicault put forward the defence that they had been married in the Scottish fashion whereby the two parties to the union had merely expressed before witnesses their desire to be man and wife. At all events, she succeeded in her divorce suit but only after

Boucicault and his new wife had returned to London and appeared together in *The Jilt*.

Soon after his last great success, *The Shaughraun*, Boucicault felt it his duty to do a more cultural type of play. 'I have given them the tweed, now I will give them the point-lace', was his new manifesto; but neither the tweed nor the point-lace seem to have been just then in fashion and he faced flop after flop.

His plans for a new Irish drama, *The O'Dowd*, which was to remove the prejudice that the Irish are 'a thriftless race of good-humoured paupers' did not win him any fresh acclaim. After his last tour in America had failed, he disbanded his company to take a job in a school of acting in Madison Square Gardens, at fifty dollars a week. He also lectured which gave him material for two books on acting. He died in an apartment in West 55th Street, New York, on 18 November 1890, after a career of over fifty years as an actor-dramatist.

Boucicault's dictum—'plays are not written, they are re-written'—gives a clue to his methods. He adapted and rewrote between rehearsals of his plays and between revivals of his plays, while all the time in search of another novel, French farce or historical incident on which he could exercise his undoubted talents as a theatre craftsman and dramatic re-toucher. When he hit on the idea for his famous dramatisation of *The Colleen Bawn* he wrote to his American theatre manager, Laura Keen, enclosing six steel engravings of scenes around Killarney, with an order to the scene painter to get to work on them at once, and a book of Irish melodies marking those which he wanted scored for orchestra. He added that he would have the first act finished soon and that he hoped to have the play upon the stage within a fortnight. He was as good as his word. The play opened in New York, on 29 March 1860, to become the best-known Irish play of the century.

He has been accused of plagiarism and of making a romantic hotch-potch of Gerald Griffin's story *The Collegians* by people who forget that the Colleen Bawn story has a factual background. Boucicault, of course, never bothered with first sources but he made due acknowledgement to Griffin in a programme dedication 'to the undying memory of his illustrious countryman, Gerald Griffin, whose beautiful romance *The Collegians* furnished the subject of the play'. This is refreshingly honest when compared with credits in theatre and cinema today, as there are only two passages in the play which are taken directly from the novel.

One reason for the disappearance of many of Boucicault's plays was that publication of these pieces constituted a considerable risk for the author. In the absence of any copyright protection for plays first produced in America which would save his work from rival managements in England, Boucicault found it practically impossible to collect royalties. When he first produced *Arrah na Pogue* at the Theatre Royal, Dublin, in 1864, two other Dublin theatres, the Queen's and the Prince of Wales staged *The Colleen Bawn* as rival attractions without leave or licence. He had earlier persuaded Congress in America to pass a statute investing the author of a play or the composer of a musical work with the sole right of representing it or permitting it to be presented. But Thomas Hailes Lacy, the London publisher of *The Colleen Bawn* and other Boucicault plays, prefaced copies with a note stating that 'in the absence of an International Treaty of Copyright—the dramas named on the title page are performance free'. However, in Boucicault's case, these were mainly the worries of a poacher turned gamekeeper.

Boucicault introduced other reforms in the theatre; he was the first manager to use fire-proof scenery; he introduced the box-set in his play *London Assurance*; and he reduced the length of shows from five hours to three, abolishing the custom of admitting the public for half-price after 9 p.m. He starred the play, not the actor—an equivocal reform, perhaps, in his case, as he usually figured as dramatist and star.

Unlike other actor-managers, before and since, it was Boucicault's practice to rehearse his plays and cast in the greatest detail, paying as much attention to bit-part players as to the leads. In this respect, he was the forerunner of the modern producer or director; it is interesting to note that his son Dion

George Darley Boucicault was the first producer to work regularly as a director of plays, in which he was not concerned in any other capacity. The younger Dion was resident producer for Charles Frohman Productions at the Duke of York's Theatre, London from 1902 to 1915.

Apart from his business flair, Boucicault had a keen eye for the topical. In 1859, seven days after John Brown's soul went marching on, he produced *The Octoroon or Life in Louisiana*, the first and for a long time the only play to treat slavery and the colour problem fairly seriously. Some years before, the Indian Mutiny had paved the way for his first American success with *Jessie Brown or The Relief of Lucknow*. He always tried to exploit local appeal in his adaptations. A French melodrama *Les Pauvres de Paris* was 'boucicaulted' as *The Poor of New York, The Poor of London, The Poor of Liverpool*, etc.

'I localise it for each town,' he explained, 'and hit the public between the eyes—I can spin-out these rough and tumble dramas as a hen lays eggs.'[1] When he visited Dublin with this piece in 1872, the irritative word 'poor' was dropped, probably in deference to Dublin Castle and the city of his birth, and the billing read *The Streets of Dublin*. But this did not save him from Castle interference. On his last visit to Dublin in 1881, he was not allowed to sing his own version of 'The Wearing of the Green' in *The Shaughraun* because of its rebel sentiments. This song was originally featured in *Arrah na Pogue* but it proved so popular with Irish audiences that Boucicault also included it in the later play. Many years before he had written to Disraeli demanding 'in the name of the Irish nation and the author of *The Shaughraun* the release of the Fenian prisoners sentenced to death for the blowing-up of Clerkenwell prison'.[2] But generally, like the good showman he was, he managed to keep on the right side of authority and might even be described as a social success which was some sort of an achievement for an Irish actor in those days.

As one reads of his success as a purveyor of sensation dramas,

[1] Townsend Walsh, *The Career of Dion Boucicault*, 1915, p. 108.
[2] Walsh, p. 109.

Boucicault takes on the appearance of a Houdini or a Maskelyne; bodies roped to railway lines, heroes trapped in caves with rising water, the parading of Derby winners on stage, earthquakes, volcanoes and the throwing of dubious Christians to real lions—all these were child's play to Boucicault.

Zola described him as 'the only English (sic) dramatist who was successful in Paris'. Charles Dickens, William Archer and George Bernard Shaw were admirers of his acting and his plays. The American-born novelist and playwright, Henry James, wrote:

Our drama seems fated, when it repairs to foreign parts for its types, to seek them first of all in the land of brogue and 'bulls'. A cynic might say that it is our privilege to see Irish types enough in the sacred glow of our domestic hearths, and that it is therefore rather cruel to condemn us to find them so inveterately in that consoling glamour of the footlights. But it is true that an Irish drama is always agreeably exciting; whether on account of an inherent property in the material, or because it is generally written by Mr. Boucicault, we are unable to say. *The Shaughraun* will, we suppose, have been the theatrical event of the season; and if a play was to run for four or five months there might have been a much worse one for the purpose than this. There is no particular writing in it, but there is an infinite amount of acting, of scene shifting, and of liveliness generally; and all this goes on to the tune of the finest feelings possible. Love, devotion, self-sacrifice, humble but heroic bravery, and brimming Irish bonhomie and irony, are the chords that are touched, and all for five liberal acts, with a great deal of very clever landscape painting in the background, and with Mr. Boucicault, Mr. Montagu, Mr. Becket and Miss Dyas in the foreground. For Mr. Boucicault, both as author and actor, it is a great triumph—especially as actor. His skill and shrewdness in knocking together effective situations and spinning lively dialogue are certainly commendable; but his acting is simply exquisite. One is hard cleverness, polished and flexible with use; the other is very like genius. The character of the Shaughraun is very happily fancied, but the best of the entertainment is to see the fancy that produced it still nightly playing with it. One hears it said sometimes that an actor acts with 'authority'; certainly there is rarely a higher degree of authority than this. Mr. Boucicault smiles too much, we think; he rather overdoes the softness, the amiability, the innocence of his hero; but these exaggerations perhaps only deepen the charm of his rendering; for it was his happy thought to devise a figure which should absolutely, consummately, and irresistibly please. It has pleased mightily.[3]

An occasional revival of *London Assurance* not only gladdens the hearts of old-timers but often comes as a surprise to the younger generation, who affect to despise Boucicault, when they are confronted with what Allardyce Nicoll describes as his uncanny sense of theatrical values. *The Shaughraun*, with Cyril Cusack in the part of Conn, was one of the great successes of 1967 at the Abbey Theatre, Dublin. This production by Hugh Hunt was also seen during the World Theatre Season, at the Aldwych Theatre, London, in 1968.

Boucicault will be remembered as a craftsman, a dramatic upholsterer. He retouched nothing which he did not theatrically adorn. He wrote consistently and successfully during a period when dramatic writing was at a low ebb, proving to be a sound journeyman playwright when—in Ken Tynan's phrase—'genius snoozed and the lunatic fringe had dandruff'.

To say, merely, that he is still remembered for *The Shaughraun* and a few other Irish romantic melodramas may be too harsh a judgement. Melodrama has outlived its usefulness as a term of critical abuse. It can now be seen as a phenomenon of the Industrial Revolution when thousands flocked to the popular theatres in the same way that millions of their descendants today sit before television screens to view 'Batman' or 'The Virginian'. Like the good showman he was, Boucicault gave his public just what they wanted. He wrote a dozen or more Irish plays but his interest was in Irish subjects, not in Irish theatre. He professed to be opposed to the stage Irishman of the blood and thunder school. Replying to some critics who did not admire the new stage Irishman *à la* Boucicault he wrote:

> I am not surprised that my delineation of the Irish peasant proved somewhat disappointing to the Christchurch public—that it was found wanting in the 'fire and energy' to which they have been

[3] Henry James, *The Scenic Art*, 1949, pp. 23-4.

accustomed. The fire and energy that consist of dancing about the stage in an expletive manner, and in indulging in ridiculous capers and extravagancies of language and gesture, form the materials of a clowning character, known as 'the stage Irishman' which it has been my invocation, as an artist and dramatist to abolish.[4]

He certainly did not abolish the stage Irishman but he refined him in his delineations of Conn the Shaughraun, Shaun the Post and Myles na Coppaleen. In a way, Boucicault may be said to have perpetuated a type who survives in a still recognisable but more attenuated form in plays by Shaw, Synge, Brendan Behan and other Irish playwrights. Shaw's Dick Dudgeon in *The Devil's Disciple,* his Blanco in *The Shewing Up of Blanco Posnet* owe not a little to Boucicault prototypes and to Boucicault's kind of theatre. Although Shaw used many of the conventions and devices of Victorian melodrama, he naturally eschewed such black-and-white simplifications as virtue rewarded and evil punished. In his inimitable fashion, Shaw took the hand-me-downs of Boucicault melodrama, turned them inside out and changed the cut and trimmings to meet the fashion of a new age.

In Synge's case, the influence is attested to by the playwright himself. In a review of *The Shaughraun* as staged in Dublin in 1904 Synge commented on the 'breath of native humour' in this 'traditional comedy of the Irish stage'. Indeed there is much of Conn the Shaughraun's gay abandon in many of Synge's tramps and in that romancing hero Christy Mahon, 'the only playboy of the western world'.

Sean O'Casey once played the part of Father Dolan in *The Shaughraun* long before he showed any interest in playwriting. He is indebted to Boucicault not only for some colourful phrases but for the blend of comedy and tragedy, song and dance, which are characteristic of many of the later O'Casey plays.

The more one reads Boucicault's plays and observes the situations the more one finds echoes of them elsewhere. *London Assurance,* on its recent revival by the Royal Shakespeare

[4] Robert Hogan, *Dion Boucicault,* 1969, p. 81.

Company, impressed many as a bridge between the comedy of manners of Sheridan's day and its more modern counterpart in the work of Oscar Wilde. It is by no means as memorable as its antecedents or descendants but it will remain one of the minor curiosities of drama, having been written by Boucicault when scarcely twenty years of age.

Nowadays, there are signs of a rebirth of melodrama everywhere—if it can ever be said to have died. Realism, which was expected to change everything, really altered very little. If one is to judge by many of the successful plays of today, we seem to hover theatrically somewhere between Restoration sex, without the artificial prose, and Victorian melodrama without the morals. So the boy from Gardiner Street still lives at least to this extent that whenever melodrama—any melodrama—is mentioned, one inevitably thinks of Dionysius Lardner Boucicault.

CHAPTER THREE

The Founders of the National Theatre

Against a background of national and cultural resurgence, a new concept of dramatic writing came into existence in the closing years of the last century. Hitherto, everything by way of actors or playwrights that Ireland had given to the theatre was given to the English theatre. But the new movement, although nationalistic in its impetus, was idealistic in concept and artistic in its aims. It was in fact destined to bring back poetic imagination to the theatre in a distant outpost of Europe.

The sprouting of a dramatic movement was one of the signs of national growth. The early 1890s had seen the first stirrings of a literary revival. The aim was not a propagandist literature which would help political nationalism but a national literature which would be, in Yeats's phrase, freed from provincialism by an exacting criticism. The Gaelic League had been founded, in 1893, for the restoration of Irish as a spoken language. Nine years earlier, the Gaelic Athletic Association had espoused the development of native games and pastimes. In 1898, the commemoration of the Rebellion of 1798 aroused not only a desire for political separatism but for cultural independence also. Much of this ferment was a reaction against the political disillusion which followed the historic Parnell split, and a growing distrust in a Westminster Parliament for a solution of the Irish problem. None the less, there was no clear indication in the 1890s that any considerable section of the population were ready for the development of a native drama. Dublin, Belfast and Cork were visited regularly by the leading London companies. Theatregoers had become accustomed to a fare of sentimental melodrama and musical comedy. The emergence of a native dramatic movement came as a surprise in a country which was largely unprepared for innovation in the arts.

To understand how this came about it is necessary to go back to the memorable meeting of W. B. Yeats, Edward Martyn and Lady Gregory, in Duras House, Kinvara, on the shores of Galway Bay, in the year 1898 when the dramatic movement which later gave us the Abbey Theatre first took shape.

W. B. Yeats was born in 1865 in Sandymount, Dublin, the son of a distinguished Irish portrait painter, J. B. Yeats. Being brought up among painters and those interested in the arts, the son studied art for a time. But the impulse towards poetry was stronger and he began to write while still a very young man. His early 'prentice works in dramatic form, *The Island of Statues* and *Mosada*, were not Irish in subject matter or manner. At this stage, the young poet was under the baleful influence of post-romantic nineteenth century verse. From boyhood, he knew intimately his mother's county, Sligo, where he became acquainted with the legends and tales of the heroic past.

His first play on an Irish subject. *The Countess Cathleen* published in 1892, was written long before he gained any practical knowledge of the theatre. The story has the directness of a medieval morality play. It is a time of famine in Ireland and the Countess sells her soul to some merchants to relieve the sufferings of her serfs. Here we have a basic situation, the struggle between good and evil. But beneath the Christian overlay there is the older and more knotty wood of Pagan tradition. The opening scene captures the legendary mood beautifully:

Mary: What can have made the grey hen flutter so?
(*Teigue, a boy of fourteen, is coming in with turf, which he lays beside the hearth.*)
Teigue: They say that now the land is famine-struck
The graves are walking.

Mary: What can the hen have heard?
Teigue: And that is not the worst; at Tubber-vannach
A woman met a man with ears spread out
And they moved up and down like a bat's wing.
Mary: What can have kept your father all this while?
Teigue: Two nights ago at Carrick-orus churchyard,
A herdsman met a man who had no mouth,
Nor eyes, nor ears, his face a wall of flesh;
He saw him plainly by the light of the moon.
Mary: Look out, and tell me if your father's coming.
(Teigue goes to door.)
Teigue: Mother!
Mary: What is it?
Teigue: In the bush beyond,
There are two birds—if you can call them birds
I could not see them rightly for the leaves—
And they've the shape and colour of horned owls,
And I'm half certain they've a human face.
Mary: Mother of God, defend us!
Teigue: They're looking at me,
What is the good of praying? father says
God and the Mother of God have dropped asleep.
What do they care, he says, though the whole land
Squeal like a rabbit under a weasel's tooth?
Mary: You'll bring misfortune with your blasphemies
Upon your father, or yourself or me.
Would God that he were home.

When the Countess Cathleen enters, the legendary mood is enhanced by the lyrical quality.

Cathleen: God save all here. There is a certain house,
An old grey castle with a kitchen garden,
A cider orchard and a plot for flowers
Somewhere among the woods.
Mary: We know it lady
A place that's set among impassable walls
As though the world's trouble could not find it out.
Cathleen: It may be that we are that trouble, for we—
Although we've wandered in the wood this hour—
Have lost it too, yet I should know my way,

	For I lived all my life in that house.
Mary:	Then you are Countess Cathleen?
Cathleen:	And this woman
	Oona, my nurse, should have remembered it,
	For we were happy for a long time there.
Oona:	The paths are overgrown with thickets now,
	Or else some change has come upon my sight.
	And this young man, that should have known the woods—
	Because we met him on the border but now,
	Wandering and singing like a wave of the sea
	Is so wrapped up in dreams of terrors to come
	That he can give no help.

The young man whom the Countess met 'wandering and singing like the wave of the sea' is the poet, Aleel, who becomes her lover. He remains a shadowy, indeterminate character, the creation of a lyrical poet, not of a dramatist. The character is so nebulous that the part was first played by an actress, Florence Farr, who may have been chosen because she could play the psaltery. Aleel, a poet from the pre-Christian Ireland of the Druids, is ill at ease within the confines of medieval morality. Apart from Cathleen's bargaining for the demon's gold and the final transformation scene, there are no developing situations which would have helped to sustain the main action. Moreover, the structure of the play with its multiplicity of scenes and time intervals is Elizabethan. Yeats's stage directions for 'trees painted in flat colour', 'missal painting' and 'vapour full of storm and ever changing light' reveal a pre-Raphaelite predilection that can only confuse a stage-designer.

Fundamentally, despite many revisions, *The Countess Cathleen* remains an imposing dramatic poem by a young man who was still outside the theatre. It contains, however, some of the loveliest verse that Yeats has written for the theatre.

Cathleen: Bend down your faces, Oona and Aleel
        I gaze upon them as the swallow gazes
        Upon the nest under the eaves, before
        She wanders the loud waters.

And:

> He bids me go
> Where none of mortal creatures but the swan
> Dabbles, and there you would pluck the harp when the trees
> Had made a heavy shadow about our door,
> And talk among the rustling of the reeds,
> When night hunted the foolish swan away
> With stillness and pale tapers.

It was not until 1894 that Yeats had his first play produced, not in Ireland but at the Avenue Theatre, London where *The Land of Heart's Desire* was staged by Florence Farr. She had asked Yeats to write a curtain raiser to John Todhunter's play *A Comedy of Sighs*, including if possible a part for her nine-year-old niece, Dorothy Paget, who was bent on a stage career. The result was a play about a changeling child who is lured away by the sidhe or fairy people on a May Eve. There are passages of great verbal beauty:

> The wind blows out of the gates of the day,
> The wind blows over the lonely of heart,
> And the lonely of heart is withered away;
> While the faeries dance in a place apart,
> Shaking their milk-white arms in the air;
> For they hear the wind laugh and murmur and sing
> Of a land where even the old are fair,
> And even the wise are merry of tongue;
> And I heard a reed of Coolaney say—
> 'When the wind has laughed and murmured and sung,
> The lonely of heart is withered away.'

The basic conflict is again between Christianity and the Paganism which Yeats found beneath the surface of folk life. None the less, this short piece does not avoid the airy-fairy dreariness one associates with end-of-the-term plays for children.

After that production in the Avenue Theatre, Yeats became interested in the idea of an Irish Theatre. But it was not until that meeting, in Duras House in 1898, the idea began to crystallise, largely through the enthusiasm of Lady Gregory and the munificence of Edward Martyn. Yeats had become interested in the possibilities of giving Ireland a theatre something on the lines of J. T. Grein's Independent Theatre where Ibsen and Shaw had their first London productions. Not that Yeats was in those days an admirer of Ibsen or Shaw except in so far as they raised a flag for the literary and artistic drama. Ibsen's great disciple—in fact his only disciple in Ireland at the time—was Edward Martyn, a wealthy Galway landowner and aspiring playwright. Martyn and Yeats succeeded in interesting George Moore in their project. Moore, a successful realistic novelist, had written a play, *The Strike at Arlingford*, produced by the Independent Theatre in 1893. He had lived for years in Paris and had first-hand knowledge of the precursor of all these literary movements—Antoine's *Théâtre Libre*. All three were united in opposition to the theatrical conditions in London and, of course, in Dublin, which made impossible the production of plays whose character did not ensure immediate commercial success. Martyn and Moore thought of Ibsen as their master and it was their intention to do for Ireland what he had done for Norway. Yeats, having already made use of a folk-tale as material for his verse play, *The Land of Heart's Desire*, was inclined to the view that a dramatic movement in Ireland should distinguish itself from its prototypes in Bergen, Paris and London by its use of Irish legend and folklore as material for poetic drama.

Already it was possible to detect a divergence of purpose among the founders of the Irish dramatic movement. But in an appeal for funds for the new enterprise, there is no such conflict:

We propose to have performed in the spring of every year certain Celtic and Irish plays, which whatever be their degree of excellence will be written with a high ambition, and so to build up a Celtic and Irish school of dramatic literature. We hope to find in Ireland an uncorrupted and imaginative audience trained to listen by its passion for oratory, and believe that our desire to bring upon the stage the deeper thoughts and emotions of Ireland will ensure for us a tolerant welcome, and that freedom of experiment which is not found in the theatres of England, and without which no new movement in art or literature can succeed. We will show that Ireland is not the home of buffoonery and easy sentiment, as it has been represented in the past but the home of an ancient idealism. We are confident of the support of all Irish people who are weary of misrepresentation, in carrying out a work that is outside all the political questions that divide us.[1]

Some have claimed to detect the hand of Martyn, who defrayed the costs of the first productions of the Irish Literary Theatre, in that statement of policy. There is no express mention of the legendary poetic drama so dear to the heart of Yeats. But neither is there express mention of the socio-intellectual Ibsenite drama which engrossed Martyn. Perhaps the third of the founding triumvirate had played the closest hand of all—Augusta, Lady Gregory. The daughter of a landowning family, the Persses of Roxboro', Co. Galway, she was then the middle-aged widow of Sir William Gregory, a former Governor of Ceylon, whose autobiography she had edited. She had no ambitions as a writer and had never been particularly interested in the theatre. She seemed to have no axe to grind having no plays produced or unproduced. But she loved poetry, particularly the poetry of W. B. Yeats; and so she was to exert an influence on the movement that neither Yeats nor Martyn could have foreseen. Lady Gregory most likely blended the oil and vinegar and launched the Irish Literary Theatre in May 1899 with productions of the plays of her partners—Yeats's poetic play *The Countess Cathleen* and Edward Martyn's *The Heather Field*, a play in the Ibsen manner.

Edward Martyn was born at Masonbrook, Loughrea, Co. Galway. His mother, Annie Smith, 'a pure peasant' as George Moore liked to call her, was the daughter of a prosperous farmer who was able to give her a dowry of her own weight in gold on her marriage to John Martyn of Tulira, a Catholic landlord descended from one Oliver Martyn, a Crusader. After schooling at Belvedere, Beaumont, and Oxford, Edward

[1] Lady Gregory, *Our Irish Theatre*, 1913, pp. 8–9.

Martyn got to know his cousin, George Moore, of Moore Hall in Mayo, a descendant of another family of Catholic landlords who claimed descent from Sir—now Saint—Thomas More. So began a strange friendship which is unforgettably and mischievously chronicled in Moore's trilogy *Hail and Farewell*. This engaging blend of fact and fiction so characteristic of the memoirs and confessions of the bizarre and brilliant Moore tells us considerably less than the whole truth about 'dear Edward'.

In two plays, *The Dream Physician* and *Romulus and Remus*, Martyn tried to retaliate against the envenomed shafts of Moore's trilogy; but honest Edward with a blackthorn was no match for the French-trained fencing master from Moore Hall. Were it not for Martyn, Moore might never have come back to Tulira and to Ireland and never have 'caught sight of Cathleen Ni Houlihan in the dusk over against the Burren mountains'. In a few revealing passages at the end of *Salve*, we get a glimpse of something approaching affection: 'There is no doubt that I owe a great deal of happiness to Edward; all my life long he has been exquisite entertainment.' But with Edward gone, Moore was a Don Quixote without his Sancho Panza.

Edward Martyn, one of the founders of the Irish Literary Theatre, relieved the fifty guarantors of their financial commitments and backed the venture himself. It is worth recalling that at this stage he not only paid the piper but had a large voice in calling the tune.

Martyn was one of the first to envisage the emergence of a national theatre as an integral part of the political and cultural resurgence. In 'A Plea for a National Theatre in Ireland' (published in *Samhain* 1901) he wrote:

Is it not time that our dramatic art should be placed on a national basis? ... This can only be done by instituting a school for the training of actors and actresses, a most important branch of which should be devoted to teaching them to act plays in the Irish language. ... With a company of artists such as I have described we might put before the people of Ireland native works, also the masterworks of all lands, for it is only by accustoming a public to the highest art that it can be led to appreciate art, and that dramatists may be inspired to work in a great art tradition.[2]

Martyn had taken a special interest in the Continental drama of ideas. His study of Ibsen and the play of ideas is evident in his first play *The Heather Field* but it would be a mistake to dismiss it as a derivative work, for in the principal part of Carden Tyrell, Martyn created a distinctive character of near-mystical intensity.

On its first production *The Heather Field* proved more successful than *The Countess Cathleen*, but F. H. O'Donnell in his pamphlet *Souls for Gold*, the students of the Royal University and Cardinal Logue, by their denunciations of the Yeats play may have contributed unwittingly to the *succes d'estime* of Martyn's play.

Cardinal Logue's second-hand interest in *The Countess Cathleen*—he had not read it—prompted some well-known Catholic Nationalists in the Royal University to voice objections to the unorthodox views of Yeats. It was argued that no Irishwoman would sell her soul to the devil and that there was an excess of irreverent comment on sacred subjects. It was the beginning of protest in the Irish theatre and a number of police attended the first performance to quell any student disturbers. The incident is unimportant now, except that it underlines the deep distrust of some Catholic Nationalists in the aims of the Irish Literary Theatre. Frank Hugh O'Donnell, a politician and journalist, in his pamphlet, had set a headline for greater onslaughts to come:

Mr. Yeats writes a sort of Maeterlinckish-Ibsenitish-Baudelairian drama or for what he calls drama, and labels his characters Maire, and Cathleen, and Oona, and Grania, and Diarmuid, and Conan, and Shemus, and Maurteen. He says 'the scene is in Ancient Ireland'. He might as well have gone to his dictionary for Brutus, and Antony, and Scipio, and Tullia, and Julia, and Faustina, and written, 'the scene is in Ancient Rome'. He cannot well be accused of forging a sham antique. Even had he the desire to forge, as a

[2] *Samhain*, no. 1, October 1901, pp. 14-15.

forgery it would be a failure. Tottenham Court Road never turned out anything quite so obvious in Old Baronial Furniture.

The astounding offensiveness of Mr. Yeats's productions towards the Irish Catholic Religion can be explained in this way. He is merely constructing an impossible country, with impossible priests and people, out of his own head, as the children say; and when he labels them Irish, he commits the most insulting things conceivable while he is merely achieving what he thinks a 'poetic creation'.[3]

Martyn, as the only Catholic among the founders, was disturbed by Cardinal Logue's intervention. But he accepted the assurances of a Jesuit, Father Finlay, that there was nothing in the play which might reasonably be objected to by a Catholic audience. None the less, the controversy which surrounded *The Countess Cathleen* gave Martyn an advantage in regard to public acceptance of his own plays.

In his second play, *Maeve*, Martyn applied the Ibsen technique to his interpretation of poetic idealism. Lady Gregory recalls that this was an exciting play in its day and that the Gaelic League turned up in force to the first production in February 1900 and sang 'Fainne Geal an Lae' and 'The Wearing of the Green' in Irish between the acts.

Martyn's third play, *The Tale of a Town*, a realistic piece dealing with small-town politics, was rejected by Yeats who passed it on to Moore who rewrote it none too successfully as *The Bending of the Bough*. This, in effect, ended Martyn's connection with the theatre he had done so much to establish.

It is an interesting coincidence that in the same summer, 1898, as Yeats, Lady Gregory and Martyn met to launch the Irish Literary Theatre, another even more significant meeting took place between two Russians, Stanislavsky and Nemirovich-Danchenko, in a Moscow restaurant. What was intended to be a chat about the state of the Russian Theatre lasted from two in the afternoon until six o'clock the next morning. Like their Irish counterparts, these two theatrical visionaries, dissatisfied with the contemporary theatre and its methods,

[3] Frank Hugh O'Donnell, *The Stage Irishman of the Pseudo Celtic Drama*, 1904, pp. 12–13.

decided that a reform of dramatic art could only come from the foundation of a new theatre. It is instructive to compare briefly the intentions of the Russians with those of the founders of the Irish movement. Stanislavsky was later to define the policy of what came to be known as the Moscow Art Theatre:

Our programme was revolutionary, we rebelled against the old way of acting, against affectation and false pathos, against declamation and bohemian exaggeration, against bad conventionality of production and sets, against the star system which ruined the ensemble and against the whole spirit of performance and significance of repertory.

The original manifesto of the Irish Literary Theatre, although more consciously nationalistic, showed a similar high idealism. The most significant difference between the two policies is that where the Russian innovators were mainly concerned with style in production and acting, the Irish trio placed the emphasis on the type of play which they would like to foster. This difference of approach is understandable as Yeats, Lady Gregory and Martyn came to the theatre as people interested in playwriting and with no first-hand knowledge of stagecraft or production. Stanislavsky and Danchenko, on the other hand, had served a long apprenticeship in the Moscow theatre. They had from the beginning that sense of the theatre which some years later the Fay brothers brought to the Irish dramatic movement. And it is interesting to note that both Stanislavsky and the Fays had been influenced by Antoine's *Théâtre Libre* in Paris.

Just as the Irish experiment had to overcome the handicap of inadequate stage facilities in the Antient Concert Rooms and even smaller halls in Camden Street and Molesworth Street, the Moscow Art Theatre began under even more depressing conditions: their first production was in a barn about thirty miles from Moscow on an improvised stage. The members of the company took lodgings near by, where they lived under rather primitive conditions, rehearsing every day from eleven to five, and in the evenings from eight to eleven. The discipline was almost monastic, and only the spirit of idealism and reform held the company together. The main innovation of the Moscow group was their conception of a dramatic presentation as an artistic ensemble, and the abolition of the star system came as a logical conclusion to this conception. But Stanislavsky's dictum, 'there are no small parts, only small actors', was also adopted at the Abbey, where leading players were often cast in minor roles.

None the less, it is doubtful if any producer at the Abbey has ever had the absolute control over his production and cast which Stanislavsky achieved almost from the beginning. Indeed the Irish dramatic movement had almost reached its zenith before stage-settings and presentation received the attention that was the hallmark of Stanislavsky's earliest productions.

Sixty years after the founding of the Moscow Arts Theatre, Madame Maria Knebel, who studied under Stanislavsky, visited Dublin for a production of *The Cherry Orchard* with the Abbey Company. Of her experiences she wrote: 'Everything about these Irish actors—their manners, speech and actions—were enhanced by lack of inhibition, sincerity and artistic temperament. I found everything strange and at the same time unusually familiar. I found to my pleasant surprise that, in spite of the language barrier, the emotional atmosphere was the same as if I had been working with Russian actors. There is a remarkable similarity between them and the Irish in their vital emotions, and their vivid, committed response to roles and the requirements of their art.'[4]

The bills presented by the Irish Literary Theatre in 1899 and 1900 had shown a nice balance between the play of ideas and lyrical pieces based on Irish saga and legend. But in 1901, there was an unsuccessful attempt to combine continental ideas with the Gaelic mode within the framework of the same play. W. B. Yeats and George Moore had written, in collaboration, *Diarmuid and Gráinne*, which was staged at the Gaiety Theatre in October 1901, with music by Elgar. This production, which might have been expected to reconcile the divergent ideas of

[4] *The Irish Times*, 28 January 1969, translated from *Sovietskya Cultura*.

the founders, not only widened the breach but proved conclusively that this tentative groping towards the idea of a national theatre had come up against a stone wall. It certainly brought to a full stop George Moore's connection with the Irish dramatic revival.

The literary ideals of the founders were admirable but their practical knowledge of the theatre was slight. All of the six plays presented by the Irish Literary Theatre were played by English actors and actresses directed by everybody and nobody. Even Sir Frank Benson's Shakespearean Company, which crossed from England to stage *Diarmuid and Gráinne*, could not save this mixture of Wagnerian opera and Celtic twilight. But on the night of this débâcle—and on the same bill—the first play in Irish ever to be staged in a recognised theatre was presented by a cast of amateurs directed by a little-known Dubliner, W. G. Fay. The play was *Casadh an tSugáin* (*The Twisting of the Rope*) by Douglas Hyde, who also played a part. That night the Irish Literary Theatre had died and at the same time it was reborn.

Born in Dublin in 1872, William George Fay was an electrician by trade. For a time he travelled about Ireland as an advance-man for a circus and played with professional fit-up companies on tour. He made his first stage appearance in Dublin under the name W. G. Ormonde in the Father Matthew Hall in 1891. For several years afterwards he appeared with his brother Frank, whose stage name was then Frank Evelyn, in melodramas and sketches in various Dublin halls.

Frank Fay was a fine speaker of verse and Yeats's dedication to him of *The King's Threshold* bears testimony to this. He was also an excellent teacher and at least two generations of Abbey actors were indebted to him for the clarity and vigour of their diction. Frank Fay was the first to advocate the formation of a National Theatre in the fullest sense—the staging of plays written by Irishmen with Irish actors and actresses. Of the founders of the Irish Literary Theatre, Edward Martyn, as we have noted, made a similar plea. The Fays and Edward Martyn also advocated the production of plays in the Irish language. It was a novel and revolutionary idea. Although Ireland has a literature in the Irish language stretching back for almost fifteen centuries to the early Christian period, no dramatic work in Irish existed until the end of the last century. The exclusively rural character of Gaelic culture and the decay of the old Gaelic order prevented the growth of a native drama. Before the coming of the Normans in the twelfth century, Dublin and other towns were Danish not Irish. The Irish language never dominated town life anywhere; and drama is an urban art. Further, all through the seventeenth, eighteenth and nineteenth centuries, the towns and the theatres were either the preserves of an English ruling class or under an authority sympathetic to foreign rule. The first play staged in Irish was produced by amateur members of the Gaelic League in 1900 in the town of Macroom, in West Cork, but W. G. Fay's production of *Casadh an tSugáin* at the Gaiety Theatre, Dublin, in 1901, was the first presentation of a play in Irish in a recognised theatre. George Moore had attempted to rehearse the cast of amateurs from the Keating Branch of the Gaelic League in a language which he did not know. But he soon abandoned what was for him a hopeless task. W. G. Fay knew little Irish either, but he brought to the job a measure of professional expertise and know-how. He and his brother Frank realised the importance of forming a company of Irish actors and actresses for the staging of Irish plays. The production of *Casadh an tSugáin* had brought folk-lore into the theatre. The author, Douglas Hyde, a founder of the Gaelic League had paved the way for the folk-plays and rural comedies of Lady Gregory, George Fitzmaurice and others which were to prove most popular with audiences in the years ahead.

Hyde's translations of Irish folklore, under the title *Beside the Fire*, showed his command of peasant idiom and phrase. But the publication in book form of Douglas Hyde's *Love Songs of Connacht*, in 1893, had revealed a new source for the development of a distinctive Irish mode in verse and poetic prose. That a steady flow of poetry and poetic dialogue should have its fountainhead in a bilingual publication of mainly anonymous lyrics may prove puzzling to those unaware of the many tributary streams which swell the main current of modern Irish literature and drama.

Just as some thirteen years earlier, Standish O'Grady, in his *History of Ireland*, dealing with the early sagas and bardic writings, undertook 'the reconstruction by imaginative processes of the life led by our ancestors in this country', Douglas Hyde discovered in the folk-poetry of Connacht a rich deposit of literary ore which was largely unknown to earlier writers. In his prose translations Hyde not only revealed what Yeats described as 'that beautiful English of the country people who remember too much Irish to talk like a newspaper' but demonstrated its potential as a basis for a new idiom of power and flexibility.

Neither Yeats nor Edward Martyn, in their preoccupation with the poetic drama and the intellectual play of ideas respectively, envisaged the emergence of the one distinctive strain which Ireland has contributed to world drama—the folk or peasant play. The Irish Literary Theatre saw nothing in this genre until October 1901, when Hyde's *Casadh an tSugáin* gave Dublin its first sight of the open hearth, the dresser filled with shining delph, and all the paraphernalia of the country kitchen. But it was not in its realistic setting, of course, that the peasant play was to make its distinctive contribution but in the quality of the writing which gave dialect and English as it is spoken in Ireland a new status in world drama.

Ironically enough, Yeats made his own contribution to this new drama in the following year when his first prose plays, *Cathleen Ni Houlihan* and *The Pot of Broth*, were staged by W. G. Fay's Irish National Dramatic Society. He had taken the first step in a direction which was far removed from his own ideals for a poetic drama which would be 'remote, spiritual, and ideal'. In 1903, W. G. Fay's company merged with the Irish Literary Theatre under the title The Irish National Theatre Society. The union of the two groups was both logical and desirable but it required all Yeats's negotiating skill to achieve it. One of the early casualties was AE (George Russell), poet, painter, mystic, economist, editor and pamphleteer who had been a founder member of W. G. Fay's Irish National Dramatic Company.

His only play, *Deirdre*, had shared the bill with Yeats's *Cathleen Ni Houlihan* in April 1902. Russell designed the costumes and scenery for his own play and spoke the prophecies of Cathvad the Druid off-stage. After some disagreement with Yeats about theatre policy, he resigned from the company in 1904.

It is interesting to compare *The King's Threshold*, the first poetic play written by Yeats after he had worked with the Fays, with the plays staged by the Irish Literary Theatre. The limited resources in money and material of the young and experimental company imposed a simplicity of acting and an economy in staging that served to emphasise the poetic quality of the dialogue. A prologue written for the first production of *The King's Threshold* in 1903 was not staged, according to Yeats, 'as owing to the smallness of the company, nobody could be spared to speak it'.

'We must simplify acting', wrote Yeats, 'We must get rid of everything that is restless, everything that draws the attention away from the sound of the voice, or from the few moments of intense expression, whether that expression is through the voice or through the hands.

'Just as it is necessary to simplify gesture that it may accompany speech, it is necessary to simplify both the form and colour of scenery and costume. There must be nothing unnecessary; nothing that will distract the attention from speech and movement. An art is always at its greatest when it is most human—Greek acting was great because it did all but everything with the voice, and modern acting may be great when it does everything with voice and movement. But an art which smothers these things with bad painting, with un-numerable garish colours; with emotional, restless mimicries of the surface of life, is an art of fading humanity—a decaying art.'[5]

The Fays practised what Yeats preached. *The King's Threshold* shows a structrual advance on *The Countess Cathleen* in that there is unity of action so that it can be played without a break. The poet, moreover, has got the rhythm of actual speech into his verse. There is a sparseness in the dialogue which is dramatic-

[5] *Samhain*, October 1903, p. 10.

ally effective. The opening speeches can be declaimed where a great deal of *The Countess Cathleen* can only be chanted:

King: I have called you hither
                To save the life of your great master, Seanchan
                For all day long it has flamed up or flickered
                To the fast-cooling hearth.
Oldest Pupil: When did he sicken?
                Is it a fever that is wasting him?
King: No fever or sickness. He has chosen death;
                Refusing to eat or drink, that he may
                Bring disgrace upon me; for there is a custom,
                An old and foolish custom, that if a man
                Be wronged or think that he is wronged, and starve
                Upon another's threshold till he die,
                The common people, for all time to come,
                Will raise a heavy cry against that threshold,
                Even though it be the King's.

The poet Seanchán has resolved to die by hunger because he has been slighted at Court. In the original 1903 version, the play ends with Seanchán's victory over the King and his triumphal return to a place at the Council Table. A poet who quarrels over a matter of Court etiquette or prestige is not likely to engage the complete sympathy of an audience. Yeats, despite his hieratic pose at times, did not really believe that the existence of poetry depends on its prestige at Court. He had written in the Prologue, in the words of an Old Man, 'Some think it would be a finer tale if Seanchán had died at the end of it, and the King had the guilt at his door, for that might have served the poet's cause better in the end.'

Seventeen years later, Yeats witnessed a real life situation which might be said to have been foreshadowed by that comment. Terence MacSwiney, a minor poet, playwright and Lord Mayor of Cork, died in Brixton Prison on 28 October 1920, after a seventy-four-day hunger-strike as a protest against his arrest by the British Forces in Ireland. As a tribute to MacSwiney's heroic protest, Yeats rewrote the ending of *The King's Threshold*:

Seanchán: I need no help.
   He needs no help that joy has lifted up
   Like some miraculous beast out of Ezekiel
   The man that dies has the chief part in the story—
      When I and these are dead
   We should be carried to some windy hill
   To lie there with uncovered face awhile
   That mankind and that leper there may know
   Dead faces laugh.   (*He falls and then half rises.*)
      King! King! Dead faces laugh.
               (*He dies.*)

This revised and solemn ending shows Seanchán as striving for something more than the restoration of a traditional right. Seanchán, like MacSwiney, has become a symbol of an ancient wrong.

   O silver trumpets, be you lifted up
   And cry to the great race that is come
   Long-throated swans upon the waves of time,
   Sing loudly, for beyond the wall of the world
   That race may hear our music and awake.

   Not what it leaves behind it in the light
   But what it carried with it to the dark
   Exalts the soul; nor song nor trumpet-blast
   Can call up races from the worsening world
   To mend the wrong and mar the solitude
   Of that great shade we follow to the tomb.

In 1903, Lady Gregory made her first bid for fame as a writer of folk-comedy with her one-acter, *Twenty Five*. But in October of that year, the Fays' presentation of *In the Shadow of the Glen* marked the arrival of a playwright of genius, John Millington Synge. Here was an unmistakable new voice. Combining a highly developed sense of drama with a gift for poetic dialogue, he revealed the latent possibilities of what was and still is widely accepted as an Abbey Play.

Synge was to have a decisive influence on the shaping of Irish drama. Within a few months he gave to the National Theatre its first masterpiece, *Riders to the Sea*.

CHAPTER FOUR

Synge and the Abbey Play

Born in Churchtown, Dublin, in 1871, Synge was the youngest child in a family of eight. His father, a barrister by profession, had a private income from property in the west of Ireland. His mother was the daughter of a West Cork rector, the Reverend Robert Traill, who had died from fever contracted during the Great Famine of 1847. After his father's death, Synge lived with his puritanical mother, in middle-class comfort, attending several private schools, until he entered Trinity College, Dublin.

Synge was descended from a Protestant Ascendancy family who had settled in County Wicklow. His family background was closely associated with the Big House, landlordism, eviction and the excesses of the land war. Although he lamented at times the passing of the great houses of the Ascendancy, he gradually became estranged from his family and class, preferring the country men whom he met in his travels in the Wicklow mountains to his conventional and strait-laced family and friends.

While at Trinity College he studied the Irish language and music. At this stage of his career, he made greater progress in music and it was not until he spent some years travelling on the Continent that he turned to literature.

Much has been written about his momentous meeting in Paris with W. B. Yeats who told Synge: 'Give up Paris; you will never create anything by reading Racine, and Arthur Symons will always be a better critic of French literature. Go to the Aran Islands. Live there as if you were one of the people themselves; express a life that has never found expression.' It is, however, likely that he would have been drawn to the West of Ireland sooner or later. He already knew some Irish and must have come in contact with some remnants of the living language in his rambles in Wicklow. In Paris he had also become acquainted with a group of Irish Nationalists which included Stephen MacKenna, Richard Irvine Best, Arthur Lynch, Maud Gonne and John O'Leary.

When Synge returned to Ireland, he spent much of his time in parts remote from books and the crowded life of cities. He observed rural life at first hand in the glens of Wicklow, in West Kerry and the Aran Islands. He had a receptive ear for the speech of those to whom English was more or less a foreign tongue, a people who had not, in his own phrase, 'shut their lips on poetry'.

Professor Daniel Corkery in *Synge and Anglo-Irish Literature* poses the question: how a man with Synge's upbringing and background could become a unique interpreter of a rural Ireland which was almost exclusively Catholic and largely Gaelic:

> The ingrained prejudices of the Ascendancy mind are so hard, so self-centred, so alien to the genius of Ireland, that no Ascendancy writer has ever succeeded in handling in literature the raw material of Irish life, as, say, a sculptor handles his clay. From old intimacy the sculptor's thumb assumes a quickened sensibility as the clay beats upon it; the clay seems to master him; it leads him on; this he is to do, and not that. But what if he despise the clay? If, taught of the centuries, he fears its contact, instinctively withdraws from it as one does from stuff that is not only slimy but treacherous? No Ascendancy writer has ever succeeded in creating a living picture of Irish life.[1]

Applying Corkery's tests of what distinguishes the Irish national being from the English national being, viz. (1) The Religious Consciousness of the People, (2) Irish Nationalism

[1] Daniel Corkery, *Synge and Anglo-Irish Literature*, 1931, p. 38.

and (3) The Land, Synge at first glance seems totally unfitted as an interpreter of Irish life. Yet, Corkery admits, with certain qualifications, that Synge, particularly in *Riders to the Sea* made a serious attempt to fathom the native consciousness. But political, linguistic or religious tests are not readily applicable to a dramatist of Synge's stature. Professor Corkery seems on surer ground in his analyses of the Irish novel and short story than in his comments on drama. An instance of this special pleading is that he excepts T. C. Murray and Padraic Colum from his general condemnation of what he terms 'Anglo-Irish' writers while O'Casey and the other Irish dramatists of the post-1922 period are not regarded as 'conscionable to the nation':

> The work, mostly amateur, done for the Abbey Theatre between 1902 and 1922 was for Ireland's self; it was, *in intention* genuine Anglo-Irish literature but more than that one cannot say. We must not be waylaid into thinking that because it shed for the nonce its Colonial character it became genuine Anglo-Irish literature, or that because the world accepts it as Irish literature, it may really turn out to be Anglo-Irish literature, or that because it is neither quite English nor quite Irish it must be Anglo-Irish.[2]

The use of the term 'Anglo-Irish' has become largely meaningless as a description of Irish writing in the English language. To say that the work of the early Abbey was, 'in intention genuine Anglo-Irish literature' merely adds to the confusion. The weakness of Corkery's case, is that a critical assessment of modern Irish drama is not possible on a solely nationalistic premise. Nationality like parentage, family, education and vocation, is something one cannot escape. Synge came closely in touch with nationalism, became an unbeliever, lived in the cabins of the Irish-speaking peasantry but he cannot be said to be representative of anybody or anything. He was, in fact, nothing but an artist.

Synge, in the preface to *The Tinker's Wedding*, like Yeats, rightly rejected the idea of literature as propaganda, but his dismissal of 'Ibsen and the Germans' as 'analysts with their

[2] Daniel Corkery, *Synge and Anglo-Irish Literature*, 1931, p. 11.

problems' is manifestly unfair not only to the author of *Peer Gynt* but to Gerhart Hauptmann, the creator of, at least, a minor masterpiece, *Hannele's Ascension*. None the less, his criticism must be considered in its context which is as follows:

The drama is made serious—in the French sense of the word—not by the degree it is taken up with problems that are serious in themselves but by the degree in which it gives the nourishment, not easy to define, on which our imaginations live. . . .

The drama, like the symphony, does not teach or prove anything. Analysts with their problems, and teachers with their systems, are soon as old-fashioned as the pharmacopoeia of Galen—look at Ibsen and the Germans—but the best of the plays of Ben Jonson and Moliere can no more go out of fashion than the blackberries on the trees.

Of the things which nourish the imagination, humour is one of the most needful, and it is dangerous to limit or destroy it. Baudelaire calls laughter the greatest sign of the Satanic element in man; and where a country loses its humour, as some towns in Ireland are doing, there will be morbidity of mind, as Baudelaire's mind was morbid.

In the greater part of Ireland, however, the whole people, from the tinkers to the clergy, have still a life, and a view of life, that is rich and genial and humorous. I do not think that these country people, who have so much humour themselves, will mind being laughed at without malice, as the people in every country have been laughed at in their own comedies.

It is interesting to note that this plea for humour and imaginative nourishment in the theatre was of no avail in his lifetime. *The Tinker's Wedding* was not produced at the Abbey until 1971 when it was included in the programmes for the Centenary of Synge's birth. Great as was his admiration for Synge, Yeats never permitted the play to be staged because he considered that the representation of the priest in this knockabout *jeu d'esprit* would offend Catholics in the audience.

Synge's knowledge of continental literature had made known to him the hidden beauty which the artist can see beneath the surface of life. In this he was at one with Yeats in his insistence that 'the restless mimicries of the surfaces of life' should be excluded from the dramatic canon. They opposed the modernist drama. The 'joyless and pallid words' of Ibsen and Zola were rejected by both.

'On the stage', wrote Synge, 'one must have reality and one must have joy; and that is why the intellectual modern drama has failed, and people have grown sick of the false joy, of the musical comedy that has been given them in place of the rich joy found only in what is superb and wild in reality. In a good play every speech should be as fully flavoured as a nut or apple, and such speeches cannot be written by anyone who works among people who have shut their lips on poetry. In Ireland, for a few years more, we have a popular imagination that is fiery, and magnificent and tender, so that those of us who wish to write start with a chance that is not given to writers in places where the spring-time of local life has been forgotten, and the harvest is a memory only, and the straw has been turned into bricks.'[3]

The founders of the National Theatre took pride in reducing everything to an ultimate simplicity. This was to be applied to stage settings, movement, gesture and speech. At one stage, Yeats played with the idea of rehearsing the cast in barrels to keep them still while they spoke their lines. Lady Gregory's idea was that they should rehearse with plates on their heads. Synge too had a hand in these practical or impractical designs. He doubtless learned much from his direct involvement with the Fays. But as far as dialogue and construction were concerned, there was little he could learn from Yeats or Lady Gregory whose dramatic skills, at this stage, were elementary. He was, however, at one with the founders in their manifesto as enunciated by Yeats in his later poem:

> John Synge, I and Augusta Gregory thought
> All that we did, all that we said or sang
> Must come from contact with the soil, from that
> Contact everything, Antaeus-like grew strong.

[3] Preface to *The Playboy of the Western World*. *The Works of J. M. Synge*, vol. II, 1910, p. 5.

> We three alone in modern times had brought
> Everything down to that sole test again,
> Dream of the noble and the beggar-man.

This idea of a theatre based upon heroic legend and peasant life was a challenge to the middle-class and cosmopolitan ideas of modernist drama. It would exclude the plays of middle-class life informed as they were by nineteenth-century optimism with its belief in progress. It was such an idea which brought Synge back from Paris to solve in his unique way the problem of how to revive poetry in a modern theatre. His dialogue was not, as he once or twice unwittingly suggested, a transcript of what he had heard among the country people of Ireland or spoken in his nursery before he could read newspapers. Synge innocently tried to explain his methods in his preface to *The Playboy of the Western World*: 'When I was writing *The Shadow of the Glen* some years ago, I got more aid than any learning could give me from the chink in the floor of a Wicklow house where I was staying, that let me hear what was being said by the servant girls in the kitchen.' This obvious simplification was eagerly seized on by his critics as an instance of how low an Ascendancy writer would stoop in his efforts to get copy about low-life downstairs. His highly stylised poetic prose is an artificial and personal medium in which he blended the English as it is spoken in Ireland with the poetic exuberance of the Elizabethans and the Jacobeans.

'All art is a collaboration', he wrote, 'and there is little doubt that in the happy ages of literature, striking and beautiful phrases were as ready to the storytellers and playwrights' hand, as the rich cloaks and dresses of his time. It is probably that when an Elizabethan dramatist took his ink-horn and sat down to his work, he used many phrases that he had just heard, as he sat at dinner, from his mother or his children. In Ireland, those of us who know the people have the same privilege.'

Synge, like Yeats, was indebted to Standish O'Grady's *History of Ireland* and his translation of saga material. He was also well aware of Douglas Hyde's pioneer work in shaping a vernacular which would make known to readers with no Irish the poetry of the country people. As Maurice Bourgeois has indicated, some of the most famous passages of poetic dialogue in *The Playboy of the Western World* have parallels in Hyde's version of *The Love Songs of Connacht*:

Hyde	Synge
I had rather be beside her on a couch kissing her ever than be sitting in heaven in the chair of the Trinity. (*Úna Bhán*)	And I squeezing kisses on your puckered lips till I'd feel a kind of pity for the Lord God is all ages sitting lonesome in his Golden Chair. (*The Playboy*)

Many other examples of casual words and phrases could be quoted; but it may be misleading to list examples as Synge must have often heard such songs and expressions on his visits to Aran and the West.

Synge was clearly conscious of Hyde's accomplishments as a translator for in a review in *The Speaker*, in 1902, of Lady Gregory's *Cuchulain of Muirthemne* he takes Yeats to task for stating in the preface that Lady Gregory was the first to use country dialect in a literary fashion pointing out that Hyde had done so much earlier in *The Love Songs*. On this point Ernest Boyd in *Ireland's Literary Renaissance* has written perceptively:

> *The Love Songs of Connacht* were the constant study of the author of *The Playboy*, whose plays testify more than any other writer, to the influence of Hyde's prose. In thus stimulating the dramatist who was to leave a deep mark on the form of the Irish theatre, Douglas Hyde must be counted an important force in the evolution of our national drama. Without injustice to the labours of W. B. Yeats, it may be said that the success of his efforts would not have been complete but for Synge. Had it not been for Hyde, the latter's most striking achievements might never have been known.[4]

But the last word must be left with Yeats who was not only a great poet but a seer, a man of vision. In 1893, the year of the

---

[4] Ernest A. Boyd, *Ireland's Literary Renaissance*, 1916, p. 79.

publication of *The Love Songs of Connacht* he concluded his review of the book with a passage which is not only remarkable for its insight but for its foreshadowing of the shape of the dramatic movement to come:

As for me, I close the book with much sadness. These poor peasants lived in a beautiful but somewhat inhospitable world where little has changed since Adam delved and Eve span. Everything was so old that it was steeped in the heart, and every powerful emotion found at once noble types and symbols for its expression. But we—we live in a world of whirling change where nothing becomes old and sacred, and our powerful emotions unless we be highly trained artists express themselves in vulgar types and symbols. . . . Yes, perhaps, this very stubborn uncomeliness of life, divorced from hill and field, has made us feel the beauty of these songs in a way the people who made them did not, despite their proverbs:
'A tune is more lasting than the song of the birds,
A word is more lasting than the riches of the world'.
We stand outside the wall of Eden and hear the trees talking together within and their talk is sweet in our ears.[5]

Synge's *In the Shadow of the Glen* is based on a story current in the folklore of many countries—how an old man, in order to spy on a giddy young wife, pretends to be dead. When she has fallen for the trap, her husband shows her the door and, as her timid lover won't go with her, she takes to the roads with a tramp.

Professor Corkery who did not like the play, describes the wife as 'a woman who wears her lusts on her sleeve'. A contemporary critic described it as 'nothing more or less than a farcical libel on the character of the average decently reared Irish peasant woman'. Both commentators cannot avoid raising moral issues which is exactly what Synge set out not to do. He did not set out 'to teach or prove anything', but to set down the thoughts and feelings of a fine young woman married to a cantankerous old man, and the fine talk of the tramp who puts into words her fear of growing old:

[5] W. B. Yeats, 'Old Gaelic Love Songs', *The Bookman*, October 1893.

Tramp (*at the door*): Come along with me now, lady of the house, and it's not my blather you'll be hearing only, but you'll be hearing the herons crying out over the black lakes, and you'll be hearing the grouse and the owls with them, and the larks and the big thrushes when the days are warm; and its not from the like of them you'll be hearing a tale of getting old like Peggy Cavanagh, and losing the hair off you, and the light of your eyes, but it's fine songs you'll be hearing when the sun goes up, and there'll be no old fellow wheezing, the like of a sick sheep, close to your ear.

Nora: I'm thinking it's myself will be wheezing that time with lying down under the heavens when the night is cold; but you've a fine bit of talk, stranger, and it's with yourself I'll go. (*She goes towards the door, then turns to Dan.*) You think it's a grand thing you're after doing with your letting on to be dead, but what is it at all? What way would a woman live in a lonesome place the like of this place, and she not making a talk with the men passing? And what way will yourself live from this day, with none to care for you? What is it you'll have now but a black life, Daniel Burke; and it's not long, I'm telling you, till you'll be lying again under that sheet, and you dead surely.

In some respects Synge's Nora is a more modern woman than Ibsen's Nora in *A Doll's House*. She has more in common with a modern existentialist than with the nineteenth-century 'emancipated' woman in revolt against bourgeois morality. The weakness of the play is that Nora's shifts of mood and feeling are at times too frequent and subtle for the compass of a one-act play.

Riders to the Sea has a classic simplicity which makes it the greatest one-act play of modern drama; an old woman sees her sixth and last son drown like his brothers. But she refuses to be broken utterly by her loss. Its economy of form and intensity of passion, has the impact of Greek tragedy. It has all the awesome power of the giant Atlantic breakers which overwhelm the men-folk of this household. But the cruel sea does not break the spirit of the mother who in her closing speeches rises above despair to a tragic serenity:

Maurya (*raising her head and speaking as if she did not see the people around her*): They're all gone now, and there isn't anything more the sea can do to me. . . . I'll have no call now to be up crying and praying when the wind breaks from the south, and you can hear the surf is in the east, and the surf is in the west, making a great stir with the two noises, and they hitting one on the other. I'll have no call now to be going down and getting Holy Water in the dark nights after Samhain, and I won't care what way the sea is when the other women will be keening. (*To Nora.*) Give me the Holy Water, Nora; there's a small sup still on the dresser. (*Nora gives it to her.*)

Maurya (*drops Michael's clothes across Bartley's feet, and sprinkles the Holy Water over him*): It isn't that I haven't prayed for you, Bartley, to the Almighty God. It isn't that I haven't said prayers in the dark night till you wouldn't know what I'd be saying; but it's a great rest I'll have now, and it's time, surely. It's a great rest I'll have now, and great sleeping in the long nights after Samhain, if it's only a bit of wet flour we do have to eat, and maybe a fish that would be stinking.

Again the reviews of the first production on 25 January 1904 were not too favourable. One paper described it as 'something like a wake'. Objections were voiced to the bringing of the drowned man's body on stage; while another paper said of it:

The latest effort of Mr. J. M. Synge depends a little on extraneous aid. There is nothing of the glorified melodrama which helps to make the popular success of other productions carried out under the auspices of the Irish National Theatre Society. In *In the Shadow of the Glen* Mr. Synge has given us so much that is beautiful and often appropriate that we were led to expect great things from the production of the one-act trifle last night.[6]

Comments such as this were but a foretaste of the vituperation which descended on Synge with the production of his major work *The Playboy of the Western World* a few years later. The production itself was notable for the discovery of a new actress, Sara Allgood, who is still remembered from later productions as an incomparable interpreter of Synge. Of her performance as Maurya some years later, a Belfast critic wrote:

[6] *Ireland's Abbey Theatre. A History*, compiled by Lennox Robinson, 1951, p. 37.

It remains in the mind as the most tragic presentation of old age that one has seen on the stage. In this bowed figure are expressed the immemorial sufferings of all who live and die by the sea, and the broken sentences are charged with an intensity of emotion that takes the spectator by the throat. The sheer art of the thing escapes one in the face of its naturalness and when the curtain drops at last one's first feeling is that of relief. It is only then that one can estimate at something like its true value the genius of the actress. While she is on the stage one is not in a theatre, but a couple of hundred miles away on the desolate western seaboard, with the din of the breakers in one's ears and the sorrow that is the heritage of generations of fisher-folk tugging at one's heart strings.[7]

Indeed to many older theatregoers at home and abroad, the names of Sara Allgood and her sister Máire O'Neill sum up the chief virtues of the Abbey style of acting. When the Fays brought Máire Nic Shiubhlaigh, Maud Gonne and other actresses from Inginidhe na hEireann (the Daughters of Erin—a Nationalist group) into the company, they did so for artistic reasons and not with a view to political propaganda. Thus the work of the Fays' Company, starting from a nationalistic basis, transcended local interest and became of international importance.

Strangely enough, it was a generous Englishwoman, Miss Annie Frederika Horniman, who ensured the continuity of the company's work by purchasing and equipping the building which became known as the Abbey Theatre and presenting it to the Irish National Theatre Society in 1904. She is said to have arrived at this momentous decision to build and subsidise a theatre in Ireland by a reading of Tarot cards and astrological charts. She was an ardent admirer of W. B. Yeats but could not agree with his co-worker, Lady Gregory. Her attitude towards the Fays and other members of the company was condescending when not openly hostile. She severed her connection with the Abbey in 1910 when the theatre failed to close its doors on the day of King Edward VII's death. Later she helped Miss Lilian Bayliss to found the Old Vic and she subsidised the

---

[7] *The Northern Whig*, 4 December 1908.

Gaiety Theatre, Manchester, where an enterprising and successful repertory theatre produced the work of Stanley Houghton and others.

Like everything new, the young Abbey was bound to meet opposition from outside and within the movement. Synge's *In the Shadow of the Glen* had aroused the ire of Arthur Griffith in *The United Irishman*. The idea of a young wife leaving an old husband, a subject as old as folklore, was seen as a libel on the peasant women of Ireland. Dudley Digges, Máire Quinn and Maud Gonne resigned from the Society in protest. Later other members of the Society left because a propagandist anti-recruiting play by Padraic Colum, *The Saxon Shilling*, had been rejected. The movement had encountered student protest from the beginning: advance denunciation of Yeats's *The Countess Cathleen* had brought some students from the old Royal University to the Antient Concert Rooms to foment rowdyism. When, in 1906, Miss Horniman endowed the theatre with an annual grant, the Society was registered as a limited liability company with a Board of Directors, consisting of Yeats, Lady Gregory and J. M. Synge, some of the leading players and members resigned in protest against what they regarded as authoritarian control.

All these protests and secessions were in the nature of a dress rehearsal for the *Playboy* row in January 1907. The acrimonious disputes carried on in the newspapers and magazines for over a decade, an argument which has not yet quite subsided, about Synge's *Playboy*, is the eternal dispute between the artist and the mob-mind. In those days, Synge was seen as a bogey-man, a drop-out, a subversive, a degenerate who defamed the Irish people. Nationalist Ireland was on the march believing in progress and that Utopia was just around the corner. Men like Arthur Griffith and D. P. Moran were hyper-sensitive to any criticism of national failings. The intelligentsia believed that Ireland was still a few hundred years behind the rest of Europe, another superior middle-class attitude to progress. Both parties were aligned to middle-class philosophy and art. The hostile reception accorded to the play is only partly accounted for by the fact that most nationalists believed that the theatre should be a propagandist medium which would advance the cause of separatism. Other objections seemed to stem from a streak of Jansenism inherent in the Catholicism of the middle classes. Cultivated people had begun to take an interest in the Irish peasant, if only as somebody who could add to the gaiety of nations. Lever, Lover, Boucicault, and Somerville and Ross set out to romanticise him and make him 'fit for a lady's chamber'. Hence the old foolishness that the Irish are happy-go-lucky and humorous, always spoiling for a fight but gentle and innocent as a turtle-dove. Hence came the stage Irishman, a swaggering good-natured buffoon who dearly loved a lord, always ready to raise a laugh or to strike a blow.

This image in time became blurred and was supplanted by the equally fallacious idea of the noble peasant who had the blood of kings in his veins. Yeats himself idealised the peasant or as he has it 'the man of roads' but he had little first-hand knowledge of how he lived or spoke. Synge came closer to the people of the Irish-speaking districts who were least influenced by foreign ways. In them, he saw a living link with the older heroic age. Synge found his imaginative stimulus not only in books but among the vagrants of Wicklow and the fishermen of Aran and the Blaskets. He sampled the folk tradition at its source. He was no sentimentalist as he revealed when he came to write *The Playboy of the Western World*.

In his most famous play, Synge deceives neither himself nor anybody else in his portrayal of the Playboy. Christy Mahon is neither a buffoon nor a fool but a gamey fellow with a touch of the poet in him kept down by a tyrannical father who treats him as an idiot born. But one day he lashes out, as even a poet will, and strikes his father with a loy, leaves him for dead and runs away. He arrives in a wild part of the West, where outlaws are still admired, and finds himself a hero, not because he is a murderer but because, if he is to live at all, he must vaingloriously tell a 'gallous story' about his dirty deed:

Christy (*very confidentially*): Up to the day I killed my father, there wasn't a person in Ireland knew the kind I was, and I there drinking, waking, eating, sleeping, a quiet, simple poor fellow with no man giving me heed.

Pegeen (*getting a quilt out of cupboard and putting it on the sack*): It was the girls were giving you heed, maybe, and I'm thinking it's most conceit you'd have to be gaming with their like.

Christy (*shaking his head, with simplicity*): Not the girls itself, and I won't tell you a lie. There wasn't anyone heeding me in that place saving only the dumb beasts of the field. (*He sits down at fire.*)

Pegeen (*with disappointment*): And I thinking you should have been living the like of a king of Norway or the eastern world. (*She comes and sits beside him after placing bread and mug of milk on the table*).

Christy (*laughing piteously*): The like of a king, is it? And I after toiling, moiling, digging, dodging from the dawn till dusk; with never a sight of joy or sport saving only when I'd be abroad in the dark night poaching rabbits on hills, for I was a divil to poach, God forgive me (*very naively*), and I near got six months for going with a dung fork and stabbing a fish.

Pegeen: And it's that you'd call sport, is it, to be abroad in the darkness with yourself alone.

Christy: I did, God help me, and there I'd be as happy as the sunshine of St. Martin's Day, watching the light passing the north or the patches of fog, till I'd hear a rabbit starting to screech and I'd go running in the furze. Then, when I'd my full share, I'd come walking down where you'd see the ducks and geese stretched sleeping on the highway of the road, and before I'd pass the dunghill, I'd hear himself snoring out—a loud, lonesome snore he'd be making all times, the while he was sleeping; and he a man'd be raging all times, the while he was waking, like a gaudy officer you'd hear cursing and damning and swearing oaths.

Pegeen: Providence and Mercy, spare us all!

There is no one so publicity conscious as a young poet. And so in his love-talk with Pegeen he is all imagination and poet's make-believe and she is all heart and good sense, all woman. Christy becomes more grandiloquent in his account of the affair when he faces a larger audience in the persons of 'the stranger girls' from over the river and the Widow Quin;

Christy (*impressively*): With that the sun came out between the cloud and the hill, and it shining green in my face. 'God have mercy on your soul,' says he, lifting a scythe. 'Or on your own,' says I, raising the loy.
Susan: That's a grand story.
Honor: He tells it lovely.
Christy (*flattered and confident, waving bone*): He gave a drive with the scythe, and I gave a lep to the east. Then I turned around with my back to the north, and I hit a blow on the ridge of his skull, laid him stretched out, and he split to the knob of his gullet.

The audience knows by now that his father, Old Mahon, is still alive, something which they only suspected in the first act. The Widow Quin, who has been mildly sceptical up to this, confronts what Christy calls 'the walking spirit of my murdered da'. From this point in the second act the action seems to sag as the audience awaits the inevitable confrontation between Christy and his father. Despite the liveliness of the racecourse episode and the magnificent love scene between Christy and Peegen Mike, the denouement is too long delayed. There is only one more strong situation when Pegeen and the others believe for a few moments that Christy has at last killed his father. Then they all turn against him, including Pegeen, though it breaks her heart.

Christy (*to Pegeen*): And what is it you'll say to me, and I after doing it this time in the face of all?
Pegeen: I'll say, a strange man is a marvel, with his mighty talk; but what's a squabble in your backyard, and the blow of a loy, have taught me that there's a great gap between a gallous story and a dirty deed. (*To men.*) Take him from this, or the lot of us will be likely put on trial for his deed today.
Christy (*with horror in his voice*): And it's yourself will send me off, to have a horny-fingered hangman hitching his bloody slip-knots at the butt of my ear.
Men (*pulling rope*): Come on, will you?
(*He is pulled down on the floor.*)
Christy (*twisting his legs round the table*): Cut the rope, Pegeen, and I'll quit the lot of you, and live from this out, like the madmen of Keel, eating muck and green weeds on the faces of the cliffs.

Pegeen: And leave us to hang, is it, for a saucy liar, the like of you?
   (*To men.*) Take him on, out from this.
Shawn: Pull a twist on his neck, and squeeze him so.
Philly: Twist yourself. Sure he cannot hurt you, if you keep your distance from his teeth alone.
Shawn: I'm afeard of him. (*To Pegeen.*) Lift a lighted sod, will you, and scorch his leg.
Pegeen (*blowing the fire with a bellows*): Leave go now, young fellow, or I'll scorch your shins.
Christy: You're blowing for to torture me. (*His voice rising and growing stronger.*) That's your kind, is it? Then let the lot of you be wary, for, if I've to face the gallows, I'll have a gay march down, I tell you, and shed the blood of some of you before I die.

When the subdued father returns on his hands and knees 'to be killed a third time' as Christy puts it, it is time for the Playboy to win a round. He is now in complete control, a gallant captain with his father for a heathen slave ready to go 'romancing through a romping lifetime—to the dawning of the judgement day'.

Like all great plays *The Playboy of the Western World* can be interpreted on several levels. It has been regarded as a political allegory of an Irish tendency to harbour and succour the wrong-doer against the forces of law and order, especially English law and order. But to say, merely, that these Mayo peasants had no politics but that they were 'agin the government' is more amusing than informative. Synge was concerned not with sociological but with imaginative realism. None the less, behind the Iron Curtain, Christy Mahon has been frequently portrayed as a Marxist revolutionary who has raised a loy, if not an army, against *petit-bourgeois* capitalism. Other advocates of social realism have noted Pegeen Mike's rebellion against the tyranny of the 'made match' which has been arranged for her with the spineless Shawneen Keogh. As the Widow Quin remarks, Pegeen is waiting on 'a sheepskin parchment to be wed with Sean Keogh of Killakeen' which suggests that, in accordance with Canon Law, she required a dispensation to marry within the forbidden degrees of kindred. The implication is that Pegeen Mike and Shawneen Keogh were first cousins; but while Synge would have been interested in inbreeding as a characteristic of rural marriages, the Canon Law requirements did not concern him.

In keeping with the ballad explosion of the 1950s, the play has been decked-out with Irish folk-tunes and presented as a ballad-opera, in Dublin and London, under the title *The Heart's a Wonder*. But even in the more orthodox and authentic Abbey productions, the play has undergone a metamorphosis. The original 'Playboy', Willie Fay, played the part in accordance with Old Mahon's description of him as 'small, black and dirty'. A later 'Playboy', Fred O'Donovan, gave Christy more of the strut and swagger of a romantic hero. Lines which were omitted during rehearsals and after the disturbances on the first night were gradually restored. Over the years, there has been a change in style of presentation and interpretation from a harsh and peasant realism to the more colourful, less naturalistic manner of an extravaganza or phantasmagoria. Herein may lie another clue to what evoked the violent protests which greeted the first production of the play on 26 January 1907.

Accounts of what actually happened during that first week of *The Playboy* in Dublin have grown to mythic proportions. Because the police were in the auditorium from the second night, the *Playboy* row got a world press which ensured the success of the play—although the protests continued for some years particularly in the United States. Nobody in the theatre during that week in Dublin could judge the play objectively, least of all the directors, author, producer and players. Despite some confusion of dates, the nearest to a dispassionate comment was written by an Englishman, Ben Iden Payne, a bird of passage:

> The night before I had been present at the opening performance of *The Playboy of the Western World* and had seen the audience (emotionally stirred by the tragic pathos of *Riders to the Sea* and hence wholly out of key at the moment with the ironic comedy of the later play) after a long, simmering, period of sporadic exclamations of opposition, boil over into a howling chorus of execration.

That had been my introduction to the public representations of the Abbey Theatre Company.

The next day, after a long discussion at the Nassau Hotel, the directors, Lady Gregory, W. B. Yeats, and J. M. Synge a little bewildered but wholly defiant decided to go on with the performance no matter how riotous the audience and even if the theatre had to be half-filled with police. Yeats had been the most resolute spokesman for the militant policy, and I remember how much I admired the far-sightedness of his assurance that it was imperative that they should assert their right at all costs in what they believed in as good art, or be forever dictated to by mob prejudice. And I remember thinking that the audience, incomprehensible as their opposition to the Playboy was to my English understanding, must be peculiarly vital or it could not have expressed its prejudice so violently. . . .[8]

Although he was stoutly defended by Yeats, Lady Gregory and the entire company in the bitter controversy which followed, Synge suffered a deep hurt. Nationalist Ireland had disowned him. P. H. Pearse, the revolutionary leader, who had learned his Irish from the same Aran islander as Synge, saw 'a sort of Evil Spirit in the shape of J. M. Synge'. Some years later, when Synge was dead, he made honourable amends when he wrote: 'When a man like Synge, a man in whose sad heart there glowed a true love of Ireland, one of the two or three men who have in our time made Ireland considerable in the eyes of the world, uses strange symbols which we do not understand, we cry out that he has blasphemed and we proceed to crucify him.'

The death of Synge, on 24 March 1909, at the early age of thirty-eight was the end of an epoch. His output was not large but he had given to the National Theatre exactly what it needed—a significant corpus of drama, distinctively Irish but with universality and depth. He laid bare the great elemental forces which throb and pulse beneath the surfaces of life. *The Well of the Saints* his somewhat neglected full-length play, treats of a sorrow that is as old as time, the evanescence of beauty and the harsh irony of reality. Martin and Mary Dhoul, two blind

---

[8] Dawson Byrne, *The Story of Ireland's National Theatre*, 1929, p. 58.

beggars, are happy as the day is long in the stained-glass world of imagination until they are cured by a saint at a holy well. The piercing light of reality only brings bitterness and disillusion; only blindness can bring back again to the beggars the many-coloured land of their dreams. Here Synge handles a theme as direct and universal as a bible parable, with a grim irony and mordant humour. The poetic prose dialogue is a perfect mirror for the beauty and ugliness which the beggars behold in their journey from darkness to light and back again. Although he uses no phrase that the beggars could not have used in daily life, Synge attempts to express what no eye has ever seen. The main fault is that the miracle itself is a cumbersome contrivance which is hardly justified by the internal development of the characters; Martin and Mary, at the final curtain, have not been affected by the action and are very much the same people as at the beginning of the play. The symbolism of Synge's first full-length play, first produced at the Abbey in February 1905, attracted the attention of Max Reinhardt who staged it in Berlin in 1906 and in Munich in 1908.

Synge's unfinished and posthumous *Deirdre of the Sorrows*, which he wrote for his beloved Máire O'Neill, is a great and tragic love-poem, based on a heroic theme. The playwright did not live to revise and complete what might have been his greatest play. It is a play of prophecy and fear. Deirdre knows from childhood that she and the sons of Usna are foredoomed to a common death. On her first meeting with her fated lover Naoise she tells him 'I am Deirdre of the Sorrows'. When the old King Conchubhar in his loneliness covets her, she dresses in her royal robes so that the prophecy may be fulfilled:

Lay out your mats and hangings where I can stand this night and look about me. Lay out the skins of the rams of Connaught and of the goats of the west. I will not be a child or a plaything; I will put on my robes that are richest, for I will not be brought down to Emain as Cuchulain brings his horse to the yoke or Conall Cearnach puts his shield upon his arm; and maybe from this day I will turn the men of Ireland like a wind blowing on the heath.

Like Cleopatra, Deirdre has immortal longings in her which she reveals in some speeches of indescribable beauty. But like most plays of prophecy, one feels that the limited action is pre-ordained and predictable. Her decision to return from Alba and safety to Emain and disaster lacks inevitability.

The language of *Deirdre of the Sorrows* is stark and bare. The luxuriance and exuberance of the Synge-song has been trimmed and shaped. The playwright's untimely death makes it difficult to say with certainty that the play marked a turning-point in his approach to drama. Daniel Corkery remarks: 'During the past hundred years from the great story of Deirdre has sprung a vast quantity of closet drama which, of all sorts of literature is certainly unreadable'.[9] He excludes from this stricture Synge's *Deirdre of the Sorrows* with the comment that it makes all other versions seem pale and weak. This seems less than fair to the Yeats version which was first staged at the Abbey in 1906. It was by all accounts a none-too-happy production. Yeats had brought Miss Darragh from England to play the lead in preference to Sara Allgood who was cast as the First Musician. Miss Darragh spoke verse in the manner of Sir Beerbohm Tree's Acting Academy while Miss Allgood and the others spoke it as Frank Fay had taught them. This one-act verse play begins where Synge commenced his last act—with the return of Deirdre and Naoise from Alba. A chorus of three musicians not only sets the scene and supplies the background story of the prophecy but is an integral part of the play. Yeats limits the scene of the action focusing the attention on what is the climax of a three-act play. The audience are plunged into the red heat of tragedy. There is an intensity and variety of mood which is lacking in his earlier verse plays. It is a fine example of Yeats's improved stagecraft. But the main characters remain remote as figures in a beautiful tapestry and lack the warm humanity of Synge's creations.

[9] Daniel Corkery, *Synge and Anglo-Irish Literature*, 1931, p. 205.

CHAPTER FIVE

Synge's Successors

The late development of a native drama in Ireland may have been a blessing in disguise. It enabled men of genius like Yeats, Synge and the Fay Brothers to break new ground in those formative years before the Abbey became a popular theatre, and so to establish a tradition which had a widespread influence at home and abroad. 'Our movement' wrote Yeats in a theatre publication *Samhain*, 'is a return to the people, like the Russian movement of the seventies . . . Plays about drawing-rooms are written for the middle classes of great cities, for the classes who live in drawing-rooms, but if you would uplift the man of the roads, you must write about the roads, or about the people of romance, or about great historical people.'[1]

This Yeatsian doctrine of a return to the people has kept Irish drama in touch with reality—the plays of Synge, Padraic Colum, Lady Gregory, George Fitzmaurice and T. C. Murray, are sufficient proof. But many will question if any people or any society can be fully expressed in so arbitrary a manner. It would be misleading to suggest that there was not loss as well as gain. Yeats's own dream of poetic theatre, remote, spiritual and ideal has hardly survived in the harsh light of realism. The step forward to a folk or peasant drama was perhaps natural and inevitable. It was understandable in a country where most town and city dwellers, rich and poor, Catholic and Protestant

[1] *Samhain*, October 1902, p. 9.

are only one or two removes from the land. Playwrights either accepted the fact or reacted acidulously to their background, like some of the best Irish novelists and writers.

'No man at all can be living forever and we must be satisfied', wrote Synge, and it will serve as his epitaph. But a creative theatre must have plays—new plays. It cannot live on revivals or in a foolish expectation of a steady succession of masterpieces. Moreover, the occasional masterpiece is not produced in a vacuum but under conditions which favour the production of original works. Synge, of course, had his imitators but no immediate successors. His style was so vigorous and individualistic that there was an obvious danger that the playwrights who came after him would be beguiled by a spurious, imitative 'Synge-song'. Just as artistic developments in music and painting have been accompanied, if not occasioned, by the discovery of some new instrument or medium, Synge's unique mastery of peasant idiom created a situation in which more than half the strength of what was and still is largely accepted as an Abbey play resided in its dialogue. But if this literary quality had not developed new modes of expression, appropriate to new subjects and themes, it would have been doomed to imitation or pastiche. That the Abbey play remained a vital and living thing after the death of Synge was largely due to his contemporaries, Lady Gregory, Padraic Colum, George Fitzmaurice and T. C. Murray, whose work, although uneven in quality, bridged the gap between Synge and the playwrights of the twenties. Although these playwrights were influenced by Synge's highly individualistic mastery of poetic prose, they developed their own individual styles and added a new dimension to the folk or peasant play, that 'first fine careless rapture' of Abbey drama.

Lady Gregory had written her first play, *Twenty Five*, when she was fifty years old; she wrote nearly forty more before her death in 1932. There was a need for comedy and she set out to supply it. She first thought of *Spreading the News* as a tragedy but as she said herself 'comedy not tragedy was wanted at our theatre to put beside high poetic work ... and I let laughter have its way with the little play'. Many of her short plays, *The Workhouse Ward*, based on a scenario by Douglas Hyde, *Hyacinth Halvey* and *Spreading the News* have a liveliness, a humour that is as Gallic as it is Gaelic. *Dervorgilla* and *The Rising of the Moon* are minor classics which display an apparent simplicity of construction that borders on genius. The last named is a perennial. A police sergeant and upholder of British rule in Ireland is watching, by a lonely quayside, for a rebel on the run. He is joined by a ballad-singer and they while away the time by singing patriotic songs which the sergeant knew before he donned the uniform. The ballads of Ireland's wrong stir some latent patriotism in the sergeant; and when it transpires that the ballad-singer is the wanted rebel in disguise, the sergeant lets him go. Nothing could be simpler or more evocative than the stage-picture: moonlight, a quayside, a barrel, a police-sergeant and a ballad-singer; and the result is magic. To three generations of playgoers the very title *The Rising of the Moon* meant the Abbey. For the first forty years of its history, the one-act play bloomed at the Abbey as in no modern theatre. A great deal of the credit for this development must go to Lady Gregory.

Her longer folk-history plays were less successful and the most interesting, *Grania*, has never been produced. It may well be that her quaint dialect, Kiltartanese—so called from a crossroads near her home at Coole, Co. Galway—is more acceptable in small doses. She spun her extravagant dialogue like tweed on a loom, yards and yards of it, flecked with fantastic colours, but often failed to cut her cloth to fit her characters. Her adaptations of Molière reveal the limitations of this dialect for translations of subtle and sophisticated classics. The Kiltartan version of *Le Bourgeois Gentilhomme* has been acidly described as a chartreuse in a churn. The fantasies *The Golden Apple*, *Aristotle's Bellows*, and *The Dragon* have a simple charm that makes them obvious material for musicals.

Her share in the prose plays of Yeats, Hyde and others has been the subject of some controversy. 'All literary collaboration is a mystery', wrote her biographer, Elizabeth Coxhead, 'but in the case of the Abbey dramatists it is less mysterious than usual because they—and particularly Lady Gregory—have left clear indications of the way they helped and were helped. Nevertheless disregarding these, waiting until she was dead and then trapping Yeats into the condoning of mis-statements in his old age, a group of literary gossips headed by the egregious Oliver St. John Gogarty succeeded in completely distorting the picture. Their efforts, which as far as I can make out, passed pretty well unchallenged in an anti-feminist country have subjected Lady Gregory's reputation to an injustice as outrageous as any that literary history can show.'[2]

Leaving aside the Women's Lib. note of her remarks, Miss Coxhead must be aware of the late Lennox Robinson's constant eulogies of the *grande-dame* of the Abbey. She knows, moreover, that Lady Gregory's short plays are produced with almost monotonous regularity in the only sphere where the one-act play claims attention today—in the amateur theatre.

Such productions are no real consolation to any discerning theatregoer who would welcome more frequent revivals under the ideal conditions which only the professional theatre can provide. But it is worth recalling that it is not only Lady Gregory's reputation which may suffer from the regrettable eclipse of the one-act form in the Irish theatre. The biographer's main contention is that the present neglect stems from the mistaken notion that Lady Gregory interfered with and spoiled Yeats's prose plays and that he really wrote the best of hers. Detecting the apparent contradiction, Miss Coxhead rightly points out that Yeats invited and acknowledged this collaboration in the case of *Cathleen Ni Houlihan* and *The Pot of Broth*. But her claim that Lady Gregory was 'the perfector of the first Anglo-Irish idiom fully adapted to literary use' will not stand up to critical examination. Indeed, there is a grain of truth in Frank O'Connor's comment that neither Lady Gregory nor Yeats could write prose dialogue that any Irish countryman really could believe in. Miss Coxhead herself provides some glaring examples by quoting such lines as 'I have the first

[2] Elizabeth Coxhead, *Lady Gregory: A Literary Portrait*, 1961, p. 105.

covetous person yet to meet I would like'. Here the 'Kiltartan infinitive' is mishandled to absurdity. Unlike Synge, T. C. Murray, or her near neighbour, Seumas O'Kelly, Lady Gregory had no mastery of dialogue that purported to be of real life. She had a feeling for the quaint and archaic and a receptive ear for 'Irish' idiom which is admirably suited to her shorter comedies.

Lady Gregory not only wrote for the Abbey, she lived for the Abbey. And when the occasion rose, she fought for the Abbey with unflinching tenacity. Her stand against Dublin Castle when there was a threat to prevent the staging of Shaw's *The Shewing-Up of Blanco Posnet* showed an exemplary courage. The play had been banned in England by the Lord Chamberlain in 1909. There never has been official stage censorship in Ireland but when the Abbey announced a production the Lord Lieutenant threatened that the theatre's patent would be revoked. Lady Gregory in her capacity of patentee of the theatre refused to consider any cuts, much to the delight of Bernard Shaw. The play was staged with great success during Horse Show Week, 1909. This made amends to Shaw for an earlier blunder when the directors refused his *John Bull's Other Island* in 1905 on the grounds that there was no actor in the Company who could play the Englishman, 'Broadbent'. Lady Gregory showed similar courage when she championed *The Playboy of the Western World* at home and abroad although it was a play she could never bring herself to like. 'She has been to me', wrote Yeats, 'mother, friend, sister and brother. I cannot realise the world without her—she brought to my wavering thoughts steadfast nobility'. Lady Gregory was as much, even more, to the Abbey Theatre.

In the first decade of this century, Padraic Colum won a considerable reputation as a dramatist. His first full-length play, *Broken Soil,*—later rewritten as *The Fiddler's House*—was produced in 1903, just a few weeks after Synge's first one-acter, *In the Shadow of the Glen*. Colum was the youngest dramatist connected with the movement in its early days, having written and published several short plays before he wrote *Broken Soil* at the age of twenty-two. Born in 1881, in Longford, where his father was Master of the Workhouse, the hushed fields of the Irish midlands seem part of Colum's consciousness.

In the three major plays of his youth, *The Land, The Fiddler's House* and *Thomas Muskerry*, Colum deals with three different aspects of country life. 'The passion for the land that motivates the first play,' writes Colum in the introduction to the latest edition, 'is not likely to be responded to in days when farms are being abandoned and when men who knew the oppression of landlordism, as Murtagh Cosgar and Martin Douras did, are not to be met with in the flesh. If staged these days, *The Land* would have to be played as an historical piece and for character parts.'

But the secondary theme of the revolt of the young against the older generation, and the resultant emigration, is only too relevant to conditions today. The tragedy, as Colum sees it, is that when the opportunity was presented of revitalising the Irish countryside, the young people were only too ready to abandon the land. It is to the young that the question is posed at the close of the play: 'Do you ever think at all of the Irish nation that is waiting all this time to be born?' Two generations of young people have been either indifferent, or have firmly answered 'No!' Perhaps for this very reason, this sincere and authentic play on an Ireland that is no more is unlikely to find an audience today.

In the second play of the trilogy, it is the artist who rebels against the tyranny of life on the land. Conn Hourican of *The Fiddler's House* is an artist by nature, and a rambler by inclination. He has tramped the roads of Ireland with his fiddle, as free as the birds, and cannot settle down to the humdrum life of a small farmer. Despite family ties, he must answer the call of the road; for 'those who have the gift must follow the gift'. In the end, he leaves his home, his family and his friends:

Well, here's Conn Hourican, the fiddler, going on his travels again. I'm leaving the house behind me, and maybe the time will come when I'll be climbing hills and seeing this house with tears in my eyes. I'm leaving the land behind me, too—but what's the land after all against the music that comes from strange places, when the night is on the ground and the bird in the grass is quiet.

This finely wrought lyrical play should be required reading for any Commission on Itinerants. No doubt some of them would find it mildly subversive, for Colum makes one conscious of that element of vagabondage in rural life to which we owe so much folk-music and folk-poetry.

In a preface to the first edition of *Thomas Muskerry* Colum discloses that he once planned 'a grandiose task, the writing of a comedy of Irish life through all the social stages'. He had shown audiences the peasant in *The Land*, the folk-artist in *The Fiddler's House*, and he then attempted a study, in the Ibsen manner, of an official in a small country town, brought to ruin by the inordinate demands of his relatives. Through the greed and insensitivity of his family, Thomas Muskerry, the Master of the Garrisowen Workhouse, ends his life in a pauper's bed in the institution over which he once ruled.

As a picture of drab and mean small-town life, the play, despite recent revision, remains unconvincing. But there are touches of greatness in the writing of the name part, and there are moments in the last act as fine as anything in Balzac's *Père Goriot*. At the close of the play, it is another man of the roads, a piper and a free man, who speaks the epitaph: 'God be good to Thomas Muskerry, the man who was good to the poor.'

When Synge died, Colum was but twenty-seven years of age. He seemed all set to become the most important dramatist in the Irish theatre. But after the production of *Thomas Muskerry* in 1910, he wrote nothing of significance for the Irish theatre for over fifty years. In his eighties, he wrote a cycle of symbolic plays on historical subjects in the Japanese 'Noh' style. Some of these, including *Moytura* and *Cloughoughter*, have been broadcast by Radio Eireann and the first-named was staged during the 1962 Dublin Theatre Festival.

It can hardly be claimed that Colum, as a dramatist lived up to the promise of his youth. Whether he was deflected from his purpose by an estrangement with the Abbey or by a greater interest in poetry, the novel and folklore, it is difficult to say. Nevertheless, his early plays have won him a place as one of the formative dramatists of the Irish Theatre.

Recent productions by the Abbey Company of *The King of the Barna Men*, *The Magic Glasses* and *The Dandy Dolls* have revived the interest of Dublin audiences in the neglected plays of George Fitzmaurice. Playgoers, somewhat belatedly, have come to recognise the unique quality of this Kerry playwright in the realm of fantasy and the grotesque.

After the death of Synge and the departure of Padraic Colum from the Abbey, George Fitzmaurice seemed destined to become one of the outstanding dramatists of the Irish theatre. His first play, *The Country Dressmaker*, first staged in 1907, the same year as *The Playboy of the Western World*, had already won him the place that William Boyle had vacated as a purveyor of kitchen-comedy. Boyle withdrew his plays from the Abbey in public protest against the staging of the *Playboy*. Fitzmaurice's second play, *The Pie-Dish*, although less popular than *The Country Dressmaker*, impressed the more discerning critics as a symbolic piece with overtones of what today would be described as black comedy. Leum Donoghue, a Kerry farmer, has worked for twenty years moulding a pie-dish. Twenty years fashioning his masterpiece and 'thirty years before that thinking about it', as he says himself. A Kerry farmer who has spent a lifetime in shaping and moulding such a useless article could hardly expect sympathy and comprehension from his family and neighbours. As a farmer, he most likely became the laughing stock of the seven parishes. Now he is dying, with the death rattle in his throat, but his only concern is to finish the pie-dish. His family are more concerned with his eternal salvation and send for the priest. But the pie-dish for Leum is the Holy Grail. The priest appeals to him to prepare his soul—but his soul is the pie-dish—his little unfinished masterpiece. The artist in Leum refuses to surrender. If God won't give him time, the devil will. He dies with a prayer to the devil on his lips and the pie-dish is smashed to smithereens on the floor. The priest pronounces his likely damnation. But his daughter is convinced that there was no sin in the foolishness of a lifetime.

As one might expect, the play was never popular. It was regarded as blasphemous, sacrilegious and grotesque. There are many parallels between the symbolism of *The Pie-Dish* and the life of George Fitzmaurice. Both Leum Donoghue and his creator strove for perfection. Both artists spent over fifty years in the attempt. Leum in the play and George in life were largely misunderstood. Neither hankered after recognition and acclaim. Both had a gift and they followed their own stars. They were essentially secretive men, labouring away at their pie-dishes in dark and gloomy rooms. They were not men of their time but 'pagans suckled in a creed outworn'.

Pie-dishes, magic glasses, dandy-dolls, became a life obsession with Fitzmaurice. He lived in the twilight world of fantasy and of the folk-imagination. He retreated into that world. Apart from his plays, we know little about him. And if anyone turns to books for information about him, he is in for some surprises. The first surprise is that his name figures in Burke's *Landed Gentry*. One would expect to find Lady Gregory there, and she is. So are Edward Martyn and George Moore. Yeats would have loved to be there but, of course, he isn't. The latest edition of Burke's *Landed Gentry* has this to say about George Fitzmaurice: the third son of the Rev. George Fitzmaurice of Bedford House, Listowel, Co. Kerry, George, born 28 January 1877, is described as playwright and actor at the Abbey Theatre, and in Hollywood films. This is as fanciful as any of his folk-tales. The man who believed that would believe anything. But genealogy apart, it is important to realize that George Fitzmaurice created his own legend. Many playwrights have fashioned wild and extravagant folk-tales into well-constructed conventional plays. *In the Shadow of the Glen*, *The Pot of Broth* and many of Lady Gregory's plays are based on folklore. But Fitzmaurice did not go to Patrick Kennedy's *Legendary Fictions of the Irish Celts*, or to Curtin or Hyde for plots. As a result, Fitzmaurice's characters leap on to the stage with an exuberance and wild abandon, as if they had suddenly broken loose from the mind of their creator. Jaymony Shanahan and his magic glasses, Roger Carmody and his dolls, the King of the Barna Men and his blue ointment are original figments of Fitzmaurice's imagination. There is nothing quite like them in modern drama except perhaps the Trolls in Ibsen's *Peer Gynt*. One can no more analyse or paraphrase the plots of these pieces than one could describe exactly a haunting dream or a violent nightmare. On one level the plots are as nonsensical as *Alice's Adventures in Wonderland* or *Snow White and the Seven Dwarfs* but we are left with a similar impression of wild tomfoolery hiding a share of common sense. Again one notes the sub-stratum of pagan belief beneath the top-soil of conventional Christianity. The Priest in *The Dandy Dolls* in search of 'his goose with the cuck on her' is every bit as much a witch doctor as the quack, Morgan Quill from Beenahorna, in *The Magic Glasses*. Modern critics will resort to a Freudian interpretation of what are essentially dream plays. They will search for sex symbols. But there is little of guilt or sin of any kind. His characters are, in the main, pure pagans. But many playgoers will baulk at such implications, and prefer to accept the fantasy plays as a glorious free-for-all where the imagination runs riot in a swirl of colour and a welter of words.

Fitzmaurice had a mastery of Kerry idiom. His dialogue owes little to Synge or other folk-dramatists. Like everything he fashioned, his language, like the 'figarios' on the pie-dish, was essentially his own. He is not equally successful in his longer plays; his realistic tragedy *The Moonlighter* and his comedy *The Country Dressmaker* show more promise than achievement. He is really a miniaturist. Fitzmaurice could carve a leprechaun on a cherry stone; he could not hew a life-size statue out of a rock.

Why, one may ask, the eclipse of a playwright who in the early years of the century seemed all set to give Irish drama a new dimension? Except for the production of a rather negligible piece, *'Twixt the Giltinans and the Carmodys*, produced at the Abbey in 1923, his work was neglected by both professionals and amateurs until the Lyric Theatre staged three of his shorter plays in the mid-forties. In an introduction to the first volume of the *Collected Plays*, the poet, Austin Clarke attributed the apparent neglect to the jealousy of Yeats and Lady Gregory:

'I happened to be in London at the time', writes Clarke, 'and I went to the Periodical Room of the British Museum and looked up in dusty files the press notices of *The Magic Glasses* when it was brought to London by the Abbey Company. My unworthy suspicion proved right. A. B. Walkley had praised the play as the best in a small repertoire, which included plays by Yeats and Lady Gregory. Other leading critics were enthusiastic. After that, *The Magic Glasses* disappeared from the Abbey stage.'

It is an interesting but implausible theory. Yeats seldom got enthusiastic notices for his plays at home or abroad in those years; but this never influenced him in providing a stage for worthwhile work or from championing the cause of any dramatist whose work he admired. Lady Gregory's help and kindness to other writers was unstinting.

A more likely explanation is that Fitzmaurice was uncertain and thin-skinned in the face of harsh Dublin criticism. He had neither the inclination nor the temperament to stand in the limelight. He had, in fact, an inordinate fear of critics and the attendant publicity. On one occasion, he allowed the Abbey actor, Eamon Kelly to stage an amateur production of *The Country Dressmaker* in the Dagg Hall on the strict understanding that no critics would be invited. On another occasion, when a radio production of *The Magic Glasses*, recorded in the authentic dialect of his native district, was planned, he would not allow a broadcast. When his Kerry neighbour and fellow-playwright, Bryan MacMahon, tried to honour him in his native Listowel, George first hid from him and then went literally 'on the run'.

In later years, it was difficult to track him down in Dublin, as he changed digs frequently. Once his landlady told an uninvited caller that Fitzmaurice had left instructions that she was to admit 'no relations and no Protestants'. This instruction had its roots in the fact that Fitzmaurice's father was a parson who married his Catholic maid, an O'Connor. Although brought up, according to the custom of the time, in the religion of his father, George feared in his old age that he might end his days in a Protestant Home for Old Men. He had only a small pension from the Department of Agriculture where he had been employed in a minor capacity.

There were, in fact, two natures at war within him—the haughty spirit of the Fitzmaurices who were once people of great power and wealth in North Kerry, and the wilder blood of the Kerry O'Connors who had been supplanted by the Fitzmaurices. Like thousands of his fellow countrymen, George joined the British Army in the First World War. Brinsley Macnamara once recalled that when George returned home on furlough, he called into the Bodega, a literary pub in those days, dressed in his uniform and was much taken aback to find that his former literary associates were too busy writing of the terrible beauty that was nineteen-sixteen to have time for the return of the hero. In later years, he hated talk of plays, particularly his own. By all accounts, it was the same story in the Department of Agriculture and in the pubs around Rathmines and Aungier Street. One had only to mention plays and he scurried for shelter.

He was found dead in a room in Harcourt Street, Dublin, in 1963. His funeral from St. Peter's, Aungier Street, to Mount Jerome was the smallest ever. George had kept to himself to the last.

Fitzmaurice lived and worked in a closed and secret world. His best work had been completed before 1914. He never quite escaped from the net which had enmeshed him in childhood. Perhaps he didn't want to escape. He continued to publish plays in *The Dublin Magazine* up to 1954. These show occasional flashes of inspiration. But one cannot but detect a steady regression and an ominous note of self-parody. It seems that before middle age, an unique but limited talent had expended itself. *The Pie-dish* remained unfinished but we can at least admire the beauty of the fragments, like shards from a Grecian Vase.

It would be a disservice to George Fitzmaurice's growing reputation to compensate for earlier neglect by indiscriminate overpraise of his work as a whole. It would be equally unwise, by allegations of jealousy on the part of Yeats and Lady Gregory, to add yet another name to the martyrology of Irish literature.

Macroom in West Cork has been picturesquely described as 'the town that never reared a fool'. As well as hard-headed businessmen, it has also produced its share of writers including the well-known Abbey playwright, Thomas Cornelius Murray.

In Murray's semi-autobiographical novel, *Spring Horizon*, there is a vivid picture of the town and the shop where he was born in 1873. The lively talk and the hard bargaining of the customers, with descriptions of countrymen as seen through the eyes of a young boy, provide some of the plots of the plays which were to come. In 1891, Murray came to St. Patrick's Training College, Drumcondra, Dublin and two years later returned as a national teacher to Carrignavar, in his native county.

Murray had been writing verse, including translations from Irish from an early age, and some of his apprentice pieces can be found in that quaint anthology, *Modern Irish Poets*, by W. J. Paul. He was also a contributor on educational topics to Father Finlay's *New Ireland Review*. His interest in drama, first awakened in his college days by study of Racine's *Athalie*, was nurtured later by visits to the Cork Opera House to see Sir Frank Benson in his seasons of Shakespeare.

Yet it was only after the establishment of the Abbey that Murray was drawn to the theatre as a writer. His first introduction to playwriting was at a little theatre modelled on the Abbey, An Dún, in Queen Street, Cork, where, in 1909, Terence McSwiney, Daniel Corkery and a local business man, Tom O'Gorman, had founded the Cork Dramatic Society for the production of plays by Munster writers. Corkery suggested to Murray that out of his experience of rural life he should attempt a play. The result was *Wheel of Fortune*, later rewritten as *Sovereign Love*, which shared the bill for 2 December 1909, with *Hermit and King* by Corkery and *The Lesson Of Life* by S. L. (afterwards Lennox) Robinson.

Recognition came quickly. His first important play, *Birthright*, produced at the Abbey in 1910, was the major offering on the opening bill when the Abbey Company made their first American appearance on 6 September 1911, at the Plymouth Theatre, Boston. The American *Playboy* riots came later and the praise for and opposition to the Murray piece was drowned in the greater tumult about a greater play. However, the American critic, Cornelius Weygandt in his *Irish Plays and Playwrights* singled out *Birthright* as the play of the year:

Many who saw *Birthright* in America were moved by it more than any other play in the repertoire of the company, and I have heard more than one, whose supreme interest is the theatre, say that it was the best play new to America presented during the winter 1911–1912.

After the first production of *Maurice Harte* by the Abbey Company at the Court Theatre, London in 1912, W. B. Yeats wrote: 'If Mr. Murray can give us more plays equal in intensity to *Maurice Harte* then we shall deserve, perhaps, as much attention as any contemporary theatre.'

After this brilliant but rather late start as a dramatist—he was thirty-seven when he got his first Abbey production—thirteen other plays succeeded *Maurice Harte*; but Yeats's rhetorical tribute quoted above prompts the question: Did Murray give us plays equal in intensity to *Maurice Harte* and, if so, did his contribution to the theatre win the attention that Yeats foresaw for Murray and the Abbey?

Frank O'Connor was of the opinion that Murray, with his mastery of West Cork dialogue, had the stuff of greatness in him, but that he was, as O'Connor put it, 'afeared of the priests'. It is scarcely an adequate explanation. It is true that after *Maurice Harte* became widely known as a play about a spoiled priest, a daring subject for a rural schoolmaster in those days, Murray had some opposition from at least one clerical manager, and that he welcomed a transfer, through the good offices of Commissioner Starkie of the Department of Education, to a Dublin school. It is also true that his one attack on the school managerial system was his unpublished play, *The Serf*, produced under the pseudonym 'Stephen Morgan'.

Murray, it should be noted, was the first realistic dramatist to write tragedies of rural life from the inside. Restraint is the keynote; the characters in his plays are neither flamboyantly romantic nor luridly brutal; and the more sensitive among them lead, in Thoreau's phrase, lives of quiet desperation. They have, like most country men most of the time, little interest in causes, just or otherwise, having troubles enough of their own and caring little for what goes on beyond the stone walls of their little mountainy farms. The themes are elemental; exile, the loveless marriage, the slavery of the hired man, the bleak years of the old, the endless vigil of mothers. Many of the plays are studies of frustration but a deep religious spirit and a brooding sense of the tears of things pierce like sunlight through the rain-drenched gloom. There are no villains, only sufferers:

> In tragic life, God wot,
> No villain need be,
> Passion spins the plot,
> We are destroyed by what is false within.

The most serious fault in Murray's writing is, perhaps, a defect of his quality as an unexcelled delineator of rural life as it was in the early years of this century. Writing from within his people, being himself so much of his people, he seems limited, at times, by some of the inhibitions of the environment he depicted. When, for instance, in his powerful tragedy *Autumn Fire* (1924), he tells us that Ellen, a farmer's daughter, has become soured and embittered because of an affair with fly-by-night, Tadhg Og, who took all her money and then deserted her, one suspects that the dramatist has told us considerably less than the whole truth. In such circumstances, farmers' daughters are more likely to lose their virtue than their money. But it says much for the writing of Ellen's part that we still believe in her bitterness despite this unconvincing reason.

Again, one feels that he might have made a more compelling play of *The Blind Wolf* had he set it in West Cork, even the

West Cork of a hundred years ago, rather than in a vague Hungarian setting which seems more suited to grand opera than to realistic tragedy. The plot is that of *The Misunderstanding* by Albert Camus, and of George Lillo's *Fatal Curiosity*, but Murray might have achieved more than either of these dramatists had he seen fit to set this grim and haunting story in the locale he knew best. In fact, Murray, has come well out of similar comparisons in the past. *Autumn Fire* has the same theme as *Desire Under the Elms*, and *Fulfilment* but it scores in its restraint over the more lurid treatments by O'Neill and the Swedish playwright Moberg.

In the mid-1920s, when Murray was at the height of his powers, he seems to have been deflected from the study of the characters and themes he knew best. About this time the idea was popular with Dublin critics and intellectuals that there was little place in the theatre for plays without a measure of international significance and that the dramatist should write about certain cosmopolitan aspects of city or urban life. Foolishly giving heed to the critics and some rivals, Murray who had written four or five eminently satisfactory plays without moving from the banks of the Sullane, attempted a more modern style of play, substituting vague experiment for inner conviction. *A Flutter of Wings*, staged by the Dublin Gate Theatre Company, attempts to contrast the freedom of the city with the narrowness of a country town; *A Stag at Bay* deals with labour troubles and strike action, and *A Spot in the Sun* has for its theme the frustration of creative talent—all three fail more from a lack of insight than from any serious faults of craftsmanship. Even *Illumination*, with a religious theme complementary to *Maurice Harte* is unconvincing and hollow; for Murray tries to substitute the chit-chat of the tennis-court and the jaded moralising of the new not-so-rich for the vigorous bargaining at the fair and Mrs. Harte's matriarchal strivings to make her son a priest.

Murray could write well only while he remained in contact with the soil. His acute ear for the undertones of West Cork speech is revealed in a dialogue pared of every excrescence which is fresh, clean cut and supple. A strong case can be made for one of his later plays, *Michaelmas Eve,* as worthy of inclusion with *Maurice Harte, Birthright* and *Autumn Fire,* as the fourth of the major tragedies. In spite of the rather contrived poisoning scene which closes the play, it has much of Murray's old mastery; there is a wild poetic surge in the dialogue with its suggestion of a more full-blooded life outside the bounds-ditch of the farm—the life of Moll Garvey's tinker clan who are always wanting the stars. But Hugh the servant-boy who loves Moll is tied like his masters to the acre of good earth and closes his ears to the call of the road.

His craftsmanship was sure from the very beginning of his long writing career. Some critics have commented on the excess of coincidence in his plots and his use of accidental happenings to motivate the action. *Spring* and *Birthright* which can be faulted in this respect, stand up remarkably well to the real test—both pieces convince an audience of their inevitability in the theatre. The catastrophe is seen to come from character; small irrelevant causes combine with the inevitable results of human frailty to achieve a tragic climax. To argue otherwise is to forget the shape of the peasant's world where little things can be all important; a band plays and a horse takes fright; a stone rolls down to crush a lamb; a cartwheel comes loose on a stony hill. These small prosaic facts are not the omens but the very instruments of tragedy.

In at least six of his fifteen published plays, Murray has left not only an authentic expression of country ways, but a profound criticism of a way of life that is fast disappearing. New tensions in the countryside today require new treatment in dramatic form, but Murray's place as a writer of tragedy seems assured; for, like the classical dramatist, he eschewed the popular and ephemeral, choosing instead the elemental themes and working them out in terms of the life he knew best. His plays may be temporarily unpopular in a changing Ireland, but his major tragedies display a sense of literature and, when given the sensitive acting which they demand, a compelling power to move an Irish audience.

CHAPTER SIX

The Abbey Style and its Influence

A London visit, in May 1903, had brought the Irish National Theatre to the notice of the London critics William Archer, Arthur Symons and Michael Field. A. B. Walkley of *The Times* commented:[1]

Stendhal said that the greatest pleasure he had ever got from the theatre was given him by performances of some poor Italian strollers in a barn. The Queen's Gate Hall, if not exactly a barn, can boast none of the glories of the ordinary playhouse; and it was there only a day or two ago a little band of Irish men and women, strangers to London and to Londoners, gave some of us who, for our sins, are constant frequenters of the regular playhouse, a few moments of calm delight quite outside the range of anything which those houses have to offer. ... As a rule they (the players) stand stock still, the speaker of the moment is the only one who is allowed a little gesture. ... The listeners do not distract one's attention by fussy stage business; they just stay where they are and listen. When they move, it is without premeditation, at haphazard, and even with a little natural clumsiness as of a people who are not conscious of being stared at in public, hence a delightful effect of spontaneity; and in their demeanour they have the artless impulsiveness of children, the very thing one found so enjoyable in another exotic affair, the performance of Sada Yacco, the Japanese actress. Add to that the Elizabethan simplicity, no more than a mere backcloth, and you will begin to see why this performance is a sight for sore eyes—eyes made sore by the perpetual movement and glitter of the ordinary stage.[1]

[1] *The Times*, May 1903.

For many years the company found it hard to live down that enthusiastic notice. Captious critics even to this day are only too ready to pounce on that word 'clumsiness' and to aver that the Abbey players were mere behaviourists, naturals, who titillated the jaded palates of London critics. What the Fays had really done was to blend the principles of the French actor Constant-Benoit Coquelin with the production methods of Antoine at the *Théâtre Libre*, and evolve a style suited to the Irish temperament. Coquelin was that *'rara avis'*, a fine actor who could bring a critical mind to the appraisal of his craft. Over a period of twenty-six years, he created the leading roles in forty-four new plays at the *Comédie Française*. After he resigned from the company, he toured England and America. One of the greatest of his later triumphs was *Cyrano de Bergerac* which Rostand wrote with Coquelin in mind. He was at his best in comic servant parts and, in this respect, his interpretations influenced the Fays and through them, Dudley Digges, Arthur Sinclair, J. M. Kerrigan, Barry Fitzgerald and, perhaps the most versatile of them all, F. J. McCormick. But if Coquelin exerted the greatest influence on the individual actors of the early Abbey, it was Antoine's *Théâtre Libre* which inspired the Fays to organise a theatre out of little more than amateur enthusiasm. Some critics of the Abbey players have described them as 'inspired amateurs', in the derogatory sense, and commented sourly that many of the players lacked intelligence and an awareness of the allied arts.

'Such intelligence,' answered Coquelin many years before, 'is a superfluous luxury; the only intelligence indispensable to the actor is that which belongs to his art. . . . An actor may be totally ignorant of painting, of music, of poetry even, and yet be a good actor and a practical actor. It is enough for him to be steeped in his own art which is different from these others.'

As a result of some ill-informed criticism of the Abbey Theatre players' 'lack of style', Miss Horniman brought over Mr. Ben Iden Payne, a Shakespearean actor to direct Wilfrid Scawen Blunt's verse play *Fand* and Maeterlinck's *Interior*. The experiment was not a success. Years afterwards Iden Payne wrote with perceptive candour:

I was imported from England at the instance of Miss A. E. F. Horniman, with a view to off-setting certain criticisms levelled against the actors on the score of 'amateurishness' and for the purpose of giving 'a more professional tone' to the productions. It soon developed, however, that the chief, and indeed the only possible accusations of amateurishness rested upon comparatively trivial points of the most external nature, such as the careless dressing of wigs and what not. Moreover, with the characteristic compromise by which I found that all relations between the company and directors and Miss Horniman, were carried on, it had been agreed that the new general manager was to have no say in regard to the peasant plays, which occupied probably nine-tenths of the performances. It was felt, and rightly, that an English producer trained in an alien technique, could not but damage that national quality the development of which was the pride and purpose of the organisation. In practice it turned out that, as an actor first and foremost, I found myself naturally taking the side of the actors in most matters of controversy even when I felt they were poor advocates for themselves, as they frequently were. ... I ask myself what was the strangest impression I carried away. It may be the prejudice of the actor recognising his own, but I find in retrospect even today that my warmest feelings of reciprocity and understanding were mainly with the actors, those fine instinctive artists, Frank and Willie Fay, Sara Allgood and Máire O'Neill, Sinclair, Kerrigan and the rest. In spite of Lady Gregory's facile pen and amusing gift for peasant farce; in spite of Yeats's keenly intellectual interest in the theatre, his critical acumen, and the loveliness of his poetry; even in spite of Synge's genius, for he was a sick man working under the sentence of death, I still feel that it was the actors—paying all deference, of course, to their dependence on the written word—to whom the theatre owed most of its vitality, even as they were individually, the most genuinely enamoured of the theatre. They were seeking no interest in the theatre; the theatre had sought and found them. They were in the theatre, and of the theatre, the hunted and not the hunters; they had been taken like a bird or a fish.[2]

[2] Dawson Byrne, *The Story of Ireland's National Theatre*, 1929, pp. 59-60.

The *Playboy* row had been fought and won, at least at home, but the Abbey was temporarily a loser. William Boyle withdrew from the Abbey his plays *The Building Fund, The Eloquent Dempsey* and *The Mineral Workers* which were among the most popular pieces in the Abbey repertoire at the time. It also caused a financial set-back which lasted for several years, because the bitter controversy dissipated the popular support which had been growing steadily since the theatre opened. It also hardened the opposition of the earlier seceders from the Company who had now founded a rival group, the Theatre of Ireland, under the chairmanship of Edward Martyn and including such important playwrights as Padraic Colum and Seumas O'Kelly and one of the greatest of the early Abbey actresses, Maire Nic Shiubhlaigh.

The most serious blow to the Theatre was the departure of the Fays early in January 1908. W. G. Fay who was producer/manager had asked Yeats to give him absolute control over the actors; in other words Fay wished to make a stipulation that Mr. Yeats should dismiss the company and let them be re-engaged personally by Mr. Fay. The Abbey directors refused to make any such concession and W. G. Fay chose to resign taking with him his wife Brigit Dempsey, his brother Frank and one or two others. This was the parting of the ways. Doubtless there was some wrong on both sides. Fay could hardly be expected to control the actors when they knew they could appeal to a higher authority. He also wished to avoid such situations as led to his apparent demotion under Ben Iden Payne. None the less, Fay's subsequent statement 'that the lavish enconomiums of the English press had been too heady for our friends, Yeats, Synge and Lady Gregory' was, to say the least, somewhat offensive to a sympathetic directorate. Likewise, his plan for the creation of a company capable of performing 'any type of play whether low life or high life, prose or verse' was clearly impractical, at that stage, when, for the first time in his brilliant career, he had lost not only the support of the directors but of most of the players as well.

When Willie and Frank Fay left the Abbey to form their own

company to present Abbey plays in New York, Chicago and elsewhere, the National Theatre, as P. S. O'Hegarty commented in 1947, 'suffered an irreparable loss, a loss which is still felt and will continue to be felt to the end of its career'. But like others of the Abbey's theatrical wild geese, Willie and Frank Fay hardly achieved the greatness which was in them on far foreign fields. In the days when a pit seat at the Abbey matinée cost only two and half new pence, Winifred M. Letts had written:

> Sixpence the passport to this splendid world
> Enchanted, sad or gay
> And you the Playboy of them all I saw
> For sixpence—Willie Fay.

At a discussion on 'Modern Irish Playwrights' at an International Theatre Seminar held at the Abbey Theatre in 1967, a distinguished director from the British National Theatre commented: 'The title doesn't make sense—if the playwrights are modern, they are not Irish, if they are Irish, they are not modern.' It is largely true that the movement was not internationally known in its early years and none of the early Abbey plays were seen on the other side of the Atlantic until 1911, when T. C. Murray's *Birthright* and Synge's *The Playboy of the Western World* infuriated Irish-American audiences. The Abbey's first date was at the Plymouth Theatre, Boston, a city with a large Irish community, where the company expected to be hailed as old friends. But the plays were either too modern or the audiences too ancient; and the players were booed and hissed. In fact, the whole cast of *The Playboy* was arrested in Philadelphia, some weeks later, and brought before a Magistrate's Court, charged with presenting immoral or indecent plays. In court, an American witness for the prosecution was asked if anything immoral had happened on the stage. Back came the reply—'Not while the curtain was up!' But in fact, the Irish-American point of view was not that much different from reactions at home where many were fiercely critical of some of the plays staged at the Abbey. The American audiences of 1911 and 1912 at least attended the plays, if only to hiss and boo. In Dublin in these years, they expressed their disapproval by staying away from the theatre, the most damning and hurtful form of criticism for a playwright and cast. But the last word on the American protests can best be left to George Bernard Shaw:

> The arrest of the Irish players is too ordinary to excite comment. All decent people are arrested in the United States—that's why I won't go. Who am I that I should question Philadelphia's right to make itself ridiculous. I warned the Irish players that America, being governed by a mysterious race, descended probably from one of the lost tribes of Israel calling themselves American Gaels, is a dangerous country for a genuine Irishman. The American Gaels are the real Playboys of the Western World.

But the riots and disturbances on that first American tour made it clear to intelligent playgoers that for the first time in its history Ireland had a theatre of its own, and a school of playwrights of its own who had set out to mirror 'the deeper thoughts and emotions of their people'. That some people at home and abroad called it a distorting mirror did not matter greatly now because gradually it became clear to audiences that what the Abbey had set out to do was to correct a falsely sentimental and romantic view of the country and its people—cottages with roses round the door, mother machrees and purty colleens in old plaid shawls, swaggering boyos with caubeens and clay-pipes—all this sunburstry, shamroguery and stage Irishry was part of what the National Theatre had set out to destroy. Plays like *Cathleen Ni Houlihan* and *The Rising of the Moon* not only gave inspiration to national bodies like the Gaelic League and Sinn Fein but foreshadowed the Insurrection of 1916. As Yeats queried, referring to *Cathleen Ni Houlihan*:

> Did that play of mine send out
> Certain men the English shot?

The first Irish casualty in the Insurrection was an Abbey actor, Sean Connolly, who was killed in an abortive attack on Dublin Castle. Ironically, he had been billed to play Peter

Gillane in a production of *Cathleen Ni Houlihan* on the Tuesday of that fateful week. The second casualty was a play billed for the same date, a first production of *The Spancel of Death* by T. H. Nally. Late on Easter Monday, the performance was cancelled because of the Insurrection. Arthur Shields, who had rehearsed T. H. Nally's play, and several other members of the company took part in the fight. *The Spancel of Death* has never been seen or scarcely heard of since. It dealt with witchcraft and superstition in eighteenth-century Mayo. T. H. Nally was a Mayo man who wrote *Finn Varra Maa*, the first Dublin pantomime based on an authentic Irish folktale. This was produced at the Theatre Royal where the performance was marred by interruptions by a pro-British section of the audience because of an excess of patriotic fervour in some of the lines. *The Spancel of Death* was one of the plays entered for the drama competition held in conjunction with the Tailteann Games in 1924. The adjudicators Lennox Robinson and James Bernard Fagan, the London playwright and impresario, included Nally's play among those highly commended. 'We praise Mr. Nally for his grim play—his treatment falls a little short of his great subject' was the joint verdict. More weight might be given to this judgement had not the same adjudicators placed T. C. Murray's *Autumn Fire* a respectable second to a forgotten one-act trifle, *The Passing*, by Kenneth Saar.

The early American tours have done more for the Abbey and for Ireland than could have been foreseen at the time. And the Abbey in return did something for the United States. For it was on seeing the company on their first American visit that the great American playwright Eugene O'Neill first felt the urge to write.

'It was seeing the Irish Players that gave me a glimpse of my opportunity,' O'Neill told an interviewer years later. 'I went to see everything they did. I thought then and I still think that they demonstrate the possibilities of naturalistic acting better than any other company.' Of *The Playboy* incidents his only recorded comment was 'The Irish can't laugh at themselves.'[3]

[3] Arthur and Barbara Gelb, *O'Neill*, 1962, p. 172.

O'Neill was proud of his Irish blood in a romantic way. The nearest he ever got to Ireland was in 1911 when the S.S. *New York* on which he had signed as an A.B. called at Cobh (then Queenstown). But shore leave was cancelled. It is hardly surprising that the Irishmen in his plays speak imitation and bogus Synge-Song.

O'Neill was particularly impressed by Synge's *Riders to the Sea* and a few years later he began to write short sea-plays for the Provincetown Players, one of the many little theatres which began to spring up all over America after the Abbey's visits. This group who later moved from Cape Cod to New York also gave Susan Glaspell her first opportunities as a playwright. Another little theatre, the Washington Square Players in Greenwich Village, began their career with a production of *The Glittering Gate*, a fantasy by Lord Dunsany. From this venture arose the prestigious New York Theatre Guild, many of whose actors and authors became internationally famous. In Chicago, Maurice Browne founded an Art Theatre on the lines of the Abbey. Synge's *Riders to the Sea* had also an impact on Bertholt Brecht who adapted it to a Spanish Civil War setting under the title *Senora Carrar's Rifles*.

However, there were more defections at home. St. John Ervine, an accomplished playwright, was a rather imperious manager for a short period. After the players had refused to be presented to Sir John Maxwell who had been in charge of the British Garrison in 1916, Ervine dismissed the entire company which included Arthur Sinclair, one of the finest character actors the Abbey ever produced. His own name was Francis Quinton McDonnell and he was the second husband of Máire O'Neill whose ill-fated romance with Synge is part of literary history. Sinclair and Máire O'Neill presented Abbey plays in England and America from 1916 to their deaths in the early 1950s. Another serious loss was the resignation of Fred O'Donovan in 1919. From his first appearance as the Boy Preacher in W. F. Casey's *The Man Who Missed the Tide*, he proved an outstanding actor with a romantic flair that brought a new dimension to such parts as Christy Mahon in *The*

Playboy. In his last two years he was manager and producer.

The most notable plays staged in those years after 1916 were St. John Ervine's *John Ferguson*, Shaw's *John Bull's Other Island*, and Lennox Robinson's comedy *The Whiteheaded Boy* and his pseudo-Parnellite play *The Lost Leader*. The seventh son of a stockbroker who took Orders in the Church of Ireland at the age of fifty, Robinson was born in Douglas, Cork. His first play, *The Clancy Name*, was produced at the Abbey in 1908. From then until his death in 1958 he was associated with the Abbey as playwright, manager and director. His best-known comedies are *The Whiteheaded Boy*, *The Far-Off Hills* and *Drama at Inish*, but his political tragedy, *The Lost Leader* contains some of his finest dialogue. He edited Lady Gregory's Journals (1946) and compiled the official history of the National Theatre (1951).

The Abbey had begun to spread its plays and its players throughout the English-speaking world. To the States went Dudley Digges, the Fay Brothers, J. M. Kerrigan, Máire O'Neill, Sara Allgood, Arthur Sinclair, Una O'Connor and, in later years, Barry Fitzgerald, his brother Arthur Shields, and many others. Of course, the cinema and nowadays television have sheltered many of the Abbey's wild geese; but while these media have made some of the players famous, it can fairly be said that success spoiled others. Any attempt to chronicle the achievements of former Abbey players in Great Britain would be an impossible and fruitless task. Nowadays, this is by no means a one-way traffic; players and directors of international repute, Siobhán McKenna, Cyril Cusack, Hugh Hunt, Tyrone Guthrie, Peter O'Toole, Eithne Dunne, Colin Blakely and Micheál MacLiammóir have appeared as guests.

Bernard Shaw was more conscious of the influence of Abbey acting than of Abbey playwriting. In a letter to an old friend, Edward McNulty, the author of the Abbey farce *The Lord Mayor*, Shaw gave some hints on the art of rehearsal. He went on to say:

The success of the Dublin Abbey Theatre was due to the fact that, when it began, none of the company was worth twopence a week for ordinary fashionable purposes, though some of them can now hold a London audience in the hollow of their hands. They were held down by Yeats and Lady Gregory ruthlessly to my formula of making the audience believe that real things were happening to real people. They were taught no tricks, because Yeats and Lady Gregory didn't know any, having found out experimentally only what any two people of high intelligence and good taste could find out by sticking to the point of securing a good representation.[4]

At home, the Abbey gradually began to find its place in the New Ireland that began to take shape after the struggle for independence. But as audiences grew, the habit of saying that the Abbey was dead or dying grew also. The accusation that the Abbey was finished is a form of attack which the theatre has had to survive for nearly seventy years. But the Abbey had the resilience and stamina to defeat black prophecy. The vision of its founders and the talent and idealism of its players and playwrights were the real assets that kept the theatre open until 1924 when the Abbey became the first State-subsidized theatre in the English-speaking world.

A tradition had been established which forced some critics to conclude that the Abbey had become part of the establishment. Since the annual government grant was first given, criticism, if anything, grew sharper. Some seemed to think that an institution in receipt of state money must, of necessity, submit to state control and that as a consequence, it was as fair a target for attack as the Government itself. Others were of the opinion that the small subsidy which alone enabled the theatre to survive, had imposed upon it the obligation to provide world theatre on a grand scale, and *avant-garde* experiment as well as continuing its avowed policy to stage new work by Irish playwrights of talent.

Not all the criticism was new or unfounded. Edward Martyn, it will be recalled, had severed his connection with the Irish Literary Theatre in 1901 after the rejection of *The Tale of a Town*. It is arguable that this decision by Yeats circumscribed the influence of the theatre movement at a crucial stage. In

[4] 'On the Art of Rehearsal', Bernard Shaw, *The Arts League of Service Annual 1921–22*, p. 4.

Martyn's case, the movement lost no masterpiece but it may have lost a valuable corrective to the artistic doctrine of a return to the people. Martyn looked to the theatre to provide the pleasures of the mind as well as the emotions of the heart; but as yet, Irish drama has failed to produce a Pirandello or a Montherlant, not to mention a Shaw, who would write 'up' rather than 'down' to the people. Yeats's own ideals for a poetic theatre had fallen on stony ground. There might have been greater hope for 'the apex of beauty' had Yeats kept Martyn at his side to fight the encroaching flood of realism.

In later years Martyn helped many different societies; the Theatre of Ireland which staged plays by Colum and Seumas O'Kelly, some of whose plays were subsequently staged at the Abbey; the National Players, who produced the rejected *The Tale of a Town*; the Players Club who produced Martyn's *The Enchanted Sea*, and the Independent Theatre Company, under Casimir Count Markiewicz, who produced his *Grangecolman*. In 1914, Martyn with the help of Thomas MacDonagh and Joseph Plunkett, both executed in 1916, founded the Irish Theatre Company which presented *The Dream Physician* in the Crane Hall, Upper O'Connell Street. Later the Irish Theatre moved to the little theatre in Hardwicke Street, an uncomfortably large Georgian room with hard chairs, where in face of rebellion and discouragement it survived for six years. Martyn's later plays, while they show flashes of an original talent, are marred by what James Joyce described as 'his incorrigible style'. It is not unfair to say that there was a sad regression from the high promise of *The Heather Field* to the footling futility of *Regina Eyre* which was Martyn's idea of a female Hamlet.

In 1914 in an article in *The Irish Review* Martyn voiced his dissatisfaction with the Abbey's policy. As this contains the germ of much subsequent criticism, it is worthy of some attention:

> After a careful examination of the material in the Abbey Theatre the fact that appears to have aided the impresarios all along is this— namely, whether intentionally or not, the type of actor and actress evolved by the undertaking is such as would be useless for making

money on the English stage. By confining themselves to acting peasants and lower middle class, they are becoming unfitted to portray the upper classes. There may possibly be exceptions in a few of the men who, having an especial talent for acting, might with study arrive at success in such parts; but the rest are hopeless. This limitation has been the strongest band (sic) for holding the company together; and to hold a company together is the chief difficulty for an impresario of the Irish theatre. Another cause of cohesion is the ill-success of the various off-shoots from the Abbey Theatre. They simply became other peasant acting companies inferior to the parent stock, and lacking the most important asset of all, the prestige of Mr. Yeats and Lady Gregory. Then the individual players who seceded at various times and could find no field on the English stage for their peculiar talents, if they did not return to the fold, sank quietly into obscurity. . . .

If I could have written capable peasant plays, which I could not because they do not interest me, in that the peasant's primitive mind is too crude for any sort of complexity of treatment, I have no doubt I should have found my place naturally in the Abbey Theatre. But I could not, and as the Abbey Theatre could not produce work like mine which was obviously not suited to their powers (they acted during one week *The Heather Field* on the whole so unsatisfactorily that they never attempted it again) I naturally became an isolated figure, who had to depend on my own efforts with amateur players of varied efficiency for seeing my dramas on the stage. . . . What is my project then? It is simply to apply the methods of the Abbey Theatre to an organisation of the most talented amateurs for the encouragement and production of native Irish drama not of the peasant species, and thereby see if, by study and perseverance, we may similarly create a school of young dramatists who will devote themselves to this particular department. I feel that, however depressed and ruined we may have been by English government and our own inept acquiescence by often playing into the hands of the enemy, we still have some inhabitants left beside peasants, and that a theatre which only treats of peasant life can never be considered, no matter how good it may be, more than a folk theatre. Consequently only partially representative of Ireland, it cannot be compared with those National Theatres in Europe which represent so completely the *minds* of the various countries where they exist. We can begin tentatively in the Abbey Theatre, if they will let us; if not, in some hall. Our plays, both native and translations of foreign masterpieces, shall be those not usually acted by professionals. We will also act plays, co-operating with the Gaelic League players, in the Irish language, from which of course, peasant subjects must not be excluded.[5]

Martyn staged the first Dublin productions of Chekhov, Strindberg and Ibsen as well as new plays by Thomas and John MacDonagh, Henry B. O'Hanlon and by himself. That there was a public, even a small one, for the productions by the Dublin Drama League, an Abbey venture launched in 1918, and by the Dublin Gate Theatre Company, in the 1930s, was largely due to Edward Martyn's Irish Theatre.

Yeats and Lennox Robinson founded the Drama League for the production of plays not normally to be seen in the commercial theatres or at the Abbey. It was intended that some of these might become part of the Abbey repertoire provided they did not interfere with its main work. The League staged productions of Pirandello, Strindberg, Chekhov, Benevente, Toller, Verhaeren, O'Neill and others. The only Irish-born authors represented were Shaw and Lord Dunsany. The plays were staged at the Abbey, with an Abbey cast, usually on Sunday and Monday nights. The performances were well attended and so something of Edward Martyn's ideas survived. Yeats, however, remained firmly of the view that even when there was a shortage of good Irish work, the Abbey should not change its policy. He felt that it was for the Irish playwrights to change their policy by a new approach to writing if a change was desirable. He believed that the creation of a second company to specialise in foreign masterpieces would be wasteful, expensive and unproductive.

Of the movements planned on the lines of the Abbey in Ireland, the Little Theatre in Cork, An Dún, produced the apprentice work of Lennox Robinson, T. C. Murray, Daniel Corkery and Terence McSwiney. The most successful, however, was the Ulster Literary Theatre. Founded in Belfast in 1904, its

[5] Edward Martyn, 'A Plea for the Revival of The Irish Literary Theatre', *The Irish Review*, April 1914, pp. 79–84.

aims were to produce literary and artistic plays which would make vital and significant the Ulster of the past, to present plays which would depict modern conditions, and to encourage a school of authors and actors. It produced plays by Joseph Campbell, Bulmer Hobson, Alice Milligan, Gerald MacNamara, Lewis Purcell and Rutherford Mayne. Unlike the Abbey, it never had a permanent home and it never received a subsidy. Rutherford Mayne later wrote two plays, *Peter* and *Bridgehead*, for the Abbey. But the most prolific playwright to come from the Ulster Theatre was George Shiels. After 1920, he became the most successful of all the Abbey playwrights.

Born in Co. Antrim, he had spent some years in America where he met with a serious accident in a railway disaster. Permanently disabled, he turned to playwriting as a substitute for playgoing and wrote some twenty plays, all but two or three of which are comedies. *The New Gossoon* and *Grogan and the Ferret* are the best examples of his sound craftsmanship, firm characterisation and lively dialogue with the bite and edge of northern speech. Of his more serious plays, *The Passing Day* and *The Rugged Path* show how this inventive writer of comedy could subdue his mood to the needs of a harsher and more sombre vision.

The Ulster Group Theatre to a large extent continued, on a more professional basis, the work of the Ulster Theatre. Among the new plays first produced by the Group were Joseph Tomelty's *Is the Priest at Home?* and John Murphy's *The Country Boy*, both of which were very successful at the Abbey. As a result of a bitter controversy over Sam Thompson's *Over the Bridge*, a realistic study of religious intolerance and sectarian strife, the Ulster Group Theatre split on the same issues that this play set out to portray.

After an initial start as a determinedly *avant-garde* theatre, the Belfast Arts Theatre, founded by Hubert Wilmot, turned to more commercial fare, having discovered at least one northern writer with a talent for the local equivalent of an Aldwych farce—Sam Cree.

The Lyric Theatre, founded by Mary O'Malley in 1951, has

remained closer to the spirit of the Ulster Literary Theatre than any of the Belfast ventures. Like its Dublin namesake, it has given a special place to the verse play, particularly the plays of Yeats.

CHAPTER SEVEN

Poetry on the Fringe

It will have been noted that the Abbey's influence at home and abroad did not greatly assist the development of poetry in the theatre. Even in the middle years, when Yeats's *On Baile's Strand* and *The Green Helmet* were frequently revived, verse drama did not flourish as Yeats would have wished. As he gained international prestige as a poet, his influence as a dramatist seemed to wane. It would be appropriate at this point to consider the reasons for this eclipse, not only in the case of Yeats but in relation to verse drama generally.

In the early 1950s when Christopher Fry's plays had a measure of success on the commercial stage in England, there was much comment in literary magazines on what was termed 'a poetic revival'. Middle-aged theatregoers will recall that there were even more sanguine hopes for a poetic revival when T. S. Eliot had considerable success with his verse plays in the 1930s and 1940s. The emergence of Eliot and Fry all but silenced the last echoes of the Stephen Phillips revival which roughly coincided with the Yeats revival in the early years of the century.

In all these cases, the word 'revival' is something of a misnomer as far as poetry in the theatre is concerned. Even in Ireland, Yeats's clarion call for a poetic drama—remote, spiritual, ideal—has become muted. As early as 1914, George Moore had pronounced the verdict: Yeats founded a realistic theatre.

His earlier heroic plays, *The Countess Cathleen*, *The King's Threshold*, *On Baile's Strand* and *Deirdre*, were bare of plot and the development is rather static. He shows little power of inventing a story; the plot is explained, not dramatised. The main elements are fine language and intensity of thought and passion. At this period, he believed that it was possible to make the poetic play a living dramatic force in the Irish theatre. He attempted to recover a lost art. The limited resources at his disposal imposed a simplicity and economy in costumes and scenery that placed the main emphasis on the verse as spoken by Florence Farr or Frank Fay. But the tide was running against him at home and abroad.

By and large, the last significant tradition of verse drama, the last sustained efforts of a succession of poets in the theatre, ended with the German Romantic Movement and the plays of Goethe, Schiller, Hebbel and Grillparzer. Prose drama, in its modern form, as distinct from the artificial prose form perfected by Congreve, Farquhar and Sheridan after the Restoration, began in 1877 with the production of Ibsen's *The Pillars of Society*. Apart from the sporadic 'revivals' mentioned above, drama in prose has ruled in the theatre ever since.

Of course, this does not mean that the poetic spirit has been excluded from the theatre for over one hundred years. Ibsen, Chekhov, Synge and, later, O'Neill and O'Casey, have gone a long way to prove that drama in prose can have an imaginative vitality which is often lacking in verse plays where the compulsion is literary rather than dramatic. For as T. S. Eliot said in his lecture, 'Poetry and Drama', at Harvard in 1950: 'If poetry is merely a decoration, an added embellishment, if it merely gives people of literary tastes the pleasures of listening to poetry at the same time that they are witnessing a play, then it is superfluous.' A great deal of Yeats's writing for the theatre had proved to be fine poetry forced into a dramatic mould. Younger and less spiritual forces were shaping the theatre he had founded. He admired the prose realists, but there were certain tendencies which clashed with his dream of recreating 'the theatre of Shakespeare or rather perhaps of Sophocles . . .'. He wanted for himself 'an unpopular theatre and an audience like a secret society where admission is by favour and never too many':

> My curse on plays
> That have to be set up in fifty ways
> On the day's war with knave and dolt,
> Theatre business, management of men.
> I swear before the dawn comes round again
> I'll find the stable and pull out the bolt.

Yeats had come to realise that there was no popular audience in Dublin or indeed in London for verse plays. He had worked hard to perfect his craft but public acceptance of his plays was marginal. Only a very small audience is available for any verse play that is not by Shakespeare. Yeats retired, as it were, from what Henry James described as the 'unholy trade'. Henceforth he would depend on the few lovers of poetry who would be content to gather in a friend's home, in a pub, or in a small hall to partake in a poetic session. Yeats probably would have ruled out the pub. Henceforth he would strive to create a theatre for himself in which he could enjoy what he called 'freedom from the stupidity of an audience'.

With that unfortunate phrase, he turned his back on his idea of a folk-theatre and 'the dream of the noble and the beggar-man'. Now it would appear that only the noble or rather the aristocracy mattered. For his first venture in a new direction, *At the Hawk's Well* was performed in March 1916, in Lady Cunard's drawing-room in London and was 'revived' shortly afterwards in Lady Islington's big drawing-room at Chesterfield Gardens 'in the presence of some three hundred fashionable people, including Queen Alexandra'.

He found his model in the aristocratic Noh drama of Japan. He would leave realism to the common people and invent 'a form of drama distinguished, indirect and symbolic, and having no need of mob or press to pay its way—an aristocratic form'. In his introduction to *Certain Noble Plays of Japan* by Ernest Fenellosa, chosen and finished by Ezra Pound, Yeats commented:

The Noh stage is a platform surrounded upon three sides by the audience. No 'naturalistic' effect is sought. The players wear masks and found their movements upon those of puppets. . . . A swift or a slow movement, and a long or short stillness and then another movement. They sing as much as they speak, and there is a chorus which describes the scene, and interprets their thoughts, and never becomes, as in the Greek theatre, a part of the action. At the climax, instead of a disordered passion of nature there is a dance, a series of positions and movements, which may represent a battle, or a marriage, or the pain of a ghost in a Buddhist purgatory.[1]

It is not at all clear why some 'three hundred fashionable people in London' should constitute a discerning audience for this exotic art form. An aristocratic art will not necessarily appeal to a fashionable audience in Lady Cunard's drawing-room or elsewhere. Whether verse drama can be preserved or revived by a return to the fourteenth-century Japan in revolt against the conventions and traditions of the Western Theatre is equally dubious. It is likely to prove as difficult as to try to revive the social and political conditions of that era. Yeats, it has been said, never leaned against a wall but he took away some of the whitewash. And he did not carry his theory of Japanese non-realism to extremes.

Although Yeats adopted the Noh form, he continued to take his themes from Irish history and legend. His most successful essay in the Noh style, *The Dreaming of the Bones*, produced at the Abbey in 1931, has an historical subject with as strong an appeal for an Irish audience as *Cathleen Ni Houlihan*. A young man, having escaped from the General Post Office, the main centre of fighting during the Insurrection of 1916, meets with the shades of Dermot MacMurrough and Dervorgilla, a pair of ill-fated lovers who are kept apart because of the memory of their great crime in first bringing the Normans to Ireland:

Young Man: What crime can stay so in the memory?
              What crime can keep apart the lips of lovers
              Wandering and alone?

[1] Introduction to *Certain Noble Plays of Japan*, 1916, pp. i–ix.

Young Girl: Her King and lover
          Was overthrown in battle by her husband,
          And for her sake and for his own, being blind
          And bitter and bitterly in love, he brought
          A foreign army from across the sea.
Young Man: You speak of Dermot and Dervorgilla
          Who brought the Norman in?
Young Girl: Yes, yes, I spoke
          Of that most miserable, most accursed pair
          Who sold their country into slavery; and yet
          They were not wholly miserable and accursed
          If somebody of their race at last would say,
          'I have forgiven them'.
Young Man: O, never, never
          Shall Dermot and Dervorgilla be forgiven.
Young Girl: If someone of their race forgave at last
          Lip would be pressed on lip.

But the ghosts appeal in vain. The young man refuses to be moved, his heart hardened by the memory of what their crime brought in its train:

Young Man: The enemy has toppled roof and gable
          And torn the panelling from ancient rooms,
          What generations of old men had known
          Like their own hands, and children wondered at,
          Has boiled a trooper's porridge.

Unforgiven, the ghosts fade away in a dance:

> They have drifted in the dance from rock to rock,
> They have raised their hands as though to snatch the sleep
> That lingers always in the abyss of the sky
> Though they can never reach it. A cloud floats up
> And covers all the mountain in a moment
> And now it lifts and they are swept away.

The sublety and elegance of this piece, so rewarding to read, would be lost in an ordinary theatre. It was a challenge to the conventions of the contemporary theatre. While the subject has all the intimacy and intensity of his prose play *Cathleen Ni Houlihan,* Yeats in *The Dreaming of the Bones* ensures that it never can have the popular appeal of that earlier piece which, as he suggested, sent out certain men the English shot. In attempting to shape a theatre for the few, he had cut himself adrift consciously if temporarily, from the dramatic movement which he had founded.

Yeats gradually became conscious of the limitations of the 'Irish Noh' play. He never in fact carried the non-realistic formula to its extreme. In his *Four Plays for Dancers* he compromised for such realistic props as a bed surrounded by real curtains and a large wooden cross. Neither did he keep his new convention in the seclusion of the drawing-room. The second of 'The Plays for Dancers', *The Only Jealousy of Emer*, was largely rewritten in prose and was produced in 1929, with the Abbey School of Ballet (choreographer Ninette de Valois) to music by George Antheil with masks by the Dutch sculptor Hilda Krop, under the title *Fighting the Waves*. It was a notable but expensive production not quite in keeping with Yeats's earlier esoteric concept. Even in their simpler form, 'The Plays for Dancers' require a perfect synthesis of three distinct arts—poetry, music, and dance. Yeats's experiments in this form had little influence in the theatre. His only disciple was another Irish poet, Padraic Colum, who, in the 1960s, wrote several short plays on historical subjects in this style.

In the last twenty years of Yeats's life, some of his most important Abbey plays were in prose. He continued to write verse plays, a few of which were produced at long intervals. But it is a regrettable but indisputable fact that Yeats's verse plays, from 1920 onwards, became very much a fringe activity in the theatre which he had founded and largely controlled until his death in 1939.

His two-act prose play, *The Player Queen*, produced at the Abbey in 1919, is an irreverent farce with delightfully odd characters. There are no noble heroes, no Cuchulain, no Deirdre. Instead there is a drunken poet, a termagent actress, a vacillating bishop, and a Prime Minister whose cure for all ills is to send somebody, anybody, to jail. It is the type of play which actors and producers invariably enjoy but which leaves an audience bewildered if amused. There are some fine pieces of rhodomontade from the drunken poet and the Player Queen out-Hecubas Hecuba. Moreover, it is one of the few Yeats plays in prose where the hand of Lady Gregory cannot be detected. Her influence is also absent from a more important play, *The Words Upon the Window Pane*, which was first produced at the Abbey in 1930. In the 1920s Yeats was preoccupied with the great prose figures of the eighteenth century, Berkeley, Goldsmith, Burke and Swift. Earlier in life he had undervalued Goldsmith and Burke, 'because they had come to seem part of the English system'. In the last years of his life he returned to them, and to Swift in particular. This preoccupation with eighteenth-century philosophy and thought is manifest in his preface to *The Words Upon the Window Pane*.

The scene is laid in a room in an eighteenth-century lodging-house on the window of which are scrawled some lines from a poem by Swift's Stella which have been identified by a student who is doing a thesis on Swift. With remarkable skill, Yeats recreates the enigma of Swift-Stella-Vanessa through a medium, Mrs. Henderson. In the course of a seance, Yeats propounds his theory of Swift's relationship with Stella and Vanessa and links it with a message from the eighteenth century for modern Ireland. The enemy, as Yeats sees it, is:

> A levelling, rancorous, rational sort of mind
> That never looked out of the eye of a saint
> Or out of a drunkard's eye.

The exposition of the theme is excellent and the craftsmanship and dialogue of this short play sustain a fine dramatic climax with Swift's cry, 'Perish the day on which I was born'. Of the performance of the part of the medium at the Abbey, Yeats commented: 'When May Craig leaves her dressing room she locks her door and leaves May Craig inside and becomes Mrs. Henderson.'

Yeats, like Shakespeare, knew little Latin and less Greek but his version of Sophocles's *Oedipus Rex* has a tragic intensity which is lacking in more scholarly translations. Written for the

Abbey Theatre where it was first produced in 1926, it was never intended as a work for the library: 'I put readers and scholars out of mind', explained Yeats in the preface, 'and wrote to be sung and spoken. The one thing that I kept in mind was that a word unfitted for living speech, out of its natural order, or unnecessary to our modern technique, would check emotion and tire attention.'

Many years earlier, Gilbert Murray had refused to prepare a stage version of this play for the Abbey. But working from the Loeb translation and with the help of Stephen MacKenna, the translator of Plotinus, Yeats eventually succeeded in preparing an eminently actable version of this great tragedy. Its success on the stage owed much to the fine acting of F. J. McCormick as Oedipus. Yeats insisted on a liturgical chant for the chorus sequences. These are the only passages in verse and they have the true Yeatsian ring. The most horrifying and violent action in the play, the death of Jocasta and the blinding of Oedipus, takes place off stage, as is customary, but Yeats's lines for the messenger serve to heighten the dramatic impact:

He struck his eyes not once but many times—the blood poured down and not with a few slow drops, but all at once over his beard in a dark shower as it were hail.

His last Abbey play, *Purgatory*, was produced in 1938, some six months before his death. Hugh Hunt's production provoked a share of controversy when an American Jesuit wanted to know what it was all about. Yeats told the press:

My plot is my meaning. I think the dead suffer remorse and re-create their old lives just as I have described. There are medieval Japanese plays about it, and much in the folklore of all countries. In my play, a spirit suffers because of its share, when alive, in the destruction of an honoured house; that destruction is taking place all over Ireland today. Sometimes it is the result of poverty, but more often because of a new individualistic generation that has lost interest in the ancient sanctities.

I know of old houses, old pictures, old furniture that have been sold without apparent regret. In a few cases a house has been destroyed by a *mésalliance*. I have founded my play on this exceptional case, partly because of my interest in certain problems of eugenics, partly because it enables me to depict more vividly than would otherwise be possible the tragedy of the house.[2]

The *mésalliance* in question was the marriage of an aristocratic lady to her groom which results in the decline of an ancient house and the degradation of a family. The product of this *mésalliance*, now an old man, has in turn begotten an ignorant and dangerous lout who has little respect for ancient pieties. The old man kills his base offspring so that guilt of his mother may be assuaged.

The play has been interpreted as an historical allegory of the rejection by modern Ireland of eighteenth-century excellence. It is a play of passion and remorse, tinged with bitter irony. Yeats had turned back to the themes of his youth but the poetic language is sparse and bare like the blasted tree which dominates the scene, a symbol of a past catastrophe.

It is convenient, at this point, to comment briefly on the fitful course of verse drama in the past three decades. It is largely true that the reign of the verse play at the Abbey died with Yeats. It also coincided with the decline in popularity of the one-act play. It was no longer possible to offer an audience a triple bill of one-acters. Occasionally a one-act verse play followed by a comedy was billed. Verse plays by F. R. Higgins, Robert Farren, Louis MacNeice and Austin Clarke have been staged at long intervals. Indeed it is significant that the best of Austin Clarke's verse plays were originally written for radio. The Dublin Verse Speaking Society, founded by Clarke and Robert Farren, had for its object the training of actors as speakers of verse particularly for broadcasting. It later developed into the Lyric Theatre Company which staged verse plays by Clarke, Donagh MacDonagh, Gordon Bottomley and Yeats.

In the past quarter-century, serious and imaginative writers such as Louis MacNeice, Archibald McLeish, Dylan Thomas and, in Ireland, Austin Clarke and Padraic Fallon have turned

[2] *The Irish Independent*, 13 August 1938.

to radio as a medium for poetic drama. Whether attracted to the fluidity and flexibility of a medium where the word is supreme or in an attempt to escape the tyranny of the box-office, these writers in verse and prose, sometimes in a mixture of both, have found a new outlet for the poetic spirit.

Austin Clarke's verse plays derive from Irish mythology, medieval satire, folklore and some minor continental drama. They display a highly individualistic blend of verbal skill and mordant humour. As a satirist, he is a master of guerrilla tactics; with unerring aim, he snipes at the present from behind the hedges of the past. In a Pierrot play, after the French of Theodore de Banville, he can write:

> All property is sacred in this land,
> When patriots can pick the public purse
> But not the private pocket, what is worse
> Than petty larceny? To rob mere pence
> And not a bank increases the offence.
> If company directors are promoted
> For fraudulence and deputies are voted
> Large pensions for possession of a rifle
> It is indictable to steal a trifle.

Even the stage directions of *The Second Kiss*, produced by the Lyric Theatre Company in 1946, are enlivened by playful mockery:

The Kiss, with which this play commences, should exceed by three seconds the emotional duration allowed by the Film censor, for there is no Irish stage censorship as yet.

In *The Irish Comic Tradition*, Vivien Mercier points out that 'very little that is worthy of satire takes place in modern Ireland without receiving its tribute in the form of a cryptic allusive poem, impregnable against lawsuits but perfectly well understood'. There is some evidence of this in his verse plays but Clarke's real strength as a satirist is to be found in his later poetry. Of course there is more than satirical overtones in the plays. Even those pieces which seem to lack a firm dramatic core are remarkable for ambidexterous rhythms and ingenious word play. *The Flame* and *Black Fast* may be described as monastic dramas in which there is a rich evocation of that dim and shadowy period which is known in the history books as the Golden Age. The Flame of St. Brigid was tended for centuries in a convent at Kildare until the custom was suppressed as superstitious by a Norman Archbishop of Dublin. *Black Fast* centres on a controversy in the early Irish Church about the exact date of Easter and when the monks should or should not undertake the penitential Lenten fasts.

Although Padraic Fallon has written two interesting stage plays, *The Seventh Step* and *Sweet Love Till Morn*, his major works, *Diarmuid and Gráinne* and *The Vision of Mac Conglinne*, were written for radio. In many respects, these two plays are the most successful modernisations of old Irish literature.

Diarmuid and Gráinne, produced by Radio Éireann in 1950, is based on the best known of all the Fianna sagas. It had already been treated in dramatic form by Yeats and George Moore in an unhappy collaboration, by Lady Gregory, and by Micheál MacLiammóir in his play in Irish. Fallon's work is neither an adaptation or redaction for radio of the saga material nor a good theatre craftsman's compression of a great tragic love story into three-act form. It is a work of intricate complexity which reveals several patterns of meaning. It has the morning freshness of the folk-tale of a beautiful young princess who, being forced to marry an old king, elopes with a young prince. But Fallon does not confine himself to a folk-treatment with strange wonders rooted in the commonplace. Combining the archaic and the colloquial, blending primeval simplicity with psychological interpretation, he fashions his material in an individualistic mould. When Diarmuid and Gráinne hide in the giant's quicken-tree in the wood of Dubhros we are imaginatively transplanted to the Garden of the Hesperides, or, if one prefers it, to the Garden of Eden itself. When Diarmuid fights the great boar of Ben Bulben, he not only shares the fate of the Greek Adonis, the Egyptian Osiris and the Cretan Zeus, but he shows a surprising Freudian insight into his unconscious. When Diarmuid plays chess with a vegetation God, the Greek

Planet—an incident not to be found in the saga, they play with the signs of the Zodiac and the game ends in geological eruptions.

These three examples are sufficient to illustrate that neither the physical nor mental action of the play can be fixed in place or time; it is not set in pre-Christian Ireland nor in an Irish other-world of pagan belief but in a mythopoeic universe where Orpheus, Jung, Sir James Frazer, Adonis, Robert Graves, Demeter, Freud and Dionysus can wander at will.

The medieval *Vision of MacConglinne*, produced by Radio Éireann in 1953, is known to Celtic Scholars, in Kuno Meyer's text, and to readers of modern Irish in An t-Athair Peadar O Laoghaire's bowdlerised version, *An Craos Deamhan*. Ligach, a Queen of Ulster, casts aside her King, Fergal, and makes overtures to Cahal, King of Munster. The Munster King becomes possessed of a mysterious and malevolent Hunger Demon and ravages the country for six months of the year, in an effort to appease his craving. His gluttony is infectious, and the stately Abbot of Cork, Muinnchenn, who attempts to exorcise the demon becomes possessed himself. Both Fergal of Ulster and the Abbot have ill-treated MacConglinne, a poet, shape-changer and goliard. But it is the poet who cures the Abbot and casts out the demon from Cahal, but only after he has been beaten, tortured and humiliated, all in service of Ligach. This brief and over-simplified synopsis can give little idea of the gusto and extravagance of Fallon's treatment. It is a blend of myth and comic spirit, of wild fancy and Rabelaisian humour. It has the satirical quality of a *Land of Cockaigne* and, on another place, a symbolic meaning, cloaked under mountains of food, which derives from the hidden harmonies of the seasons. Austin Clarke in his play *The Son of Learning*, produced at the Cambridge Festival in 1927, was content to take the story much as he found it and to embroider it with assonantal patterns. Fallon aims much higher—at cosmic significance.

Essentially a radio piece, with its quick transitions, the narrator or commentator in the play supplied the visual imagery, sometimes in verse but generally in melodic prose:

The plucks night the poor poet to the seaboard. He disappears out of ken. But one delicate morning, when the skies were watercolours of hazy blues and early sun-rays, on the bar of Wexford where a few mild monks of Ibar's community were knotting a torn herring-net, a salt-white coracle of ozier-wattles moves towards them on the tide from around Raven point. It was the wonderful golden head of the poet they noticed first. Then, as he slowly whorled past them, they saw he was green ivy to the chin, that his face was moulded like a mask of molten gold and that he lived.

Despite the occasional mystification and extravagance, the eloquence, wit and poetry of *The Vision of MacConglinne* sustain the basic story of two kings and a beautiful treacherous woman who uses a poet as her footstool.

'We have often thought,' wrote AE, 'that a book surpassing *The Arabian Nights* might be made by a writer of genius who would weld into a continuous narrative the tales of the gods, the Fianna and the Red Branch, so full of beauty, mystery and magnificence, that as raw material for romance, there is hardly anything to equal them, in the legendary literature of other countries.' Padraic Fallon has not taken AE's hint—he would hardly be interested in surpassing *The Arabian Nights*—but he has shown, in a none too fruitful period of poetic theatre, that the poet's imagination can still function with defiance and with vigour.

CHAPTER EIGHT

O'Casey and After

No sooner had the Abbey Theatre received a small government subsidy in 1924 than its critics belaboured it as part of the establishment and as 'an institution as conservative as the National Gallery or the National Museum'. But both the critics and the establishment were quickly disillusioned with the arrival of a new playwright of genius, Sean O'Casey.

Sean O'Casey was born in Dorset Street, Dublin on 30 March 1880. Though both his parents were Protestants, they were of the lower middle class and not in any way connected with the privileged Anglo-Irish ruling class. From his youth, O'Casey chose to identify himself with the Catholic working class, joined the Gaelic League and the Irish Republican Brotherhood, a separatist physical force movement. During the Transport Workers' Strike of 1913, he worked closely with the labour leader, Jim Larkin, and in the following year became Secretary of the Irish Citizen Army, a working-class revolutionary force who later took part in the Insurrection of Nineteen-Sixteen. O'Casey, however, had severed his connection with militant labour long before the Rising. Though not a participant O'Casey experienced the terror and violence of the War of Independence and the grim tragedies of Civil War in Ireland. It is against such a background that he wrote his trilogy of plays in Dublin tenement settings.

The Shadow of a Gunman, produced at the Abbey in 1923,

portrays the plight of the slum-dwellers during the Black and Tan War. The plot revolves about Seamus Shields, a loquacious pedlar, Donal Davoren, a romantic poet, and a slum-girl, Minnie Powell. Davoren, a coward at heart, is pleased to be regarded as a dangerous man, a gunman on the run. A visitor to the tenement leaves a bag in the room, and Davoren and Shields discover later that it contains bombs. The Black and Tans arrive; Minnie takes the bag to her room to save Davoren whom she admires. She is arrested and shot when she tries to escape. Davoren and Shields are ironic mouthpieces for O'Casey's reactions to this night of terror. 'The country is gone mad', exclaims Shields. 'Instead of countin' their beads now they're countin' bullets; their Hail Marys and Pater Nosters are bustin' bombs—bustin' bombs and the rattle of machine guns; petrol is their holy water; their mass is a burnin' buildin', their *De Profundis* is "The Soldiers' Song" and their creed is, I believe in the gun almighty, maker of heaven an' earth—an' it's all for the glory o' God an' the honour of Ireland.'

When Minnie Powell gives her life without demur, O'Casey identifies himself with Davoren's cry: 'Ah me, alas! Pain, pain, pain ever, for ever. It's terrible to think that little Minnie is dead, but it's still more terrible to think that Davoren and Shields are alive! Oh, Donal Davoren, shame is your portion now till the silver cord is loosened and the golden bowl be broken. Oh, Davoren, Donal Davoren, poet and poltroon, poltroon and poet!'

Here the men play the coward's exculpatory rôle while Minnie not only smuggles arms but hurls defiance at her captors in the face of death. It is a theme which O'Casey develops in a greater play, *Juno and the Paycock*, first staged at the Abbey in 1924. The action takes place during the Civil War of 1922 when the Irish Free State, recently established, engaged in a bitter struggle with the Irish Republican Army. The life of another tenement family, the Boyles, is tragically and humorously portrayed. Juno Boyle, the mother, tries to keep her family together while her husband, 'the paycock', Captain Boyle struts through the pubs by day and night with his cadging and sycophantic boon-companion, Joxer Daly. When the play opens, Mary, the daughter is on strike and Johnny, the son, is an invalid as a result of gun-shot wounds. But the dominant note is one of comedy. For the Boyles have just heard that they have inherited a legacy and begin to buy furniture on credit and to install a gramophone while they entertain the neighbours on the strength of their good fortune. But the legacy is contested and tragedy begins to close in on the Boyle family; the creditors invade the tenement room and strip it; Mary is left pregnant by her superior-like school-teacher friend, and Johnny, who has spied on a comrade, is dragged away to execution by Republican gunmen. Juno, amid the ruins, can only cry 'Sacred Heart o' Jesus take away our hearts o' stone . . . an' give us hearts o' flesh. . . . Take away this murderin' hate . . . an' give us Thine own eternal love'. Then the Captain and his butty Joxer roll home hopelessly drunk, to collapse on the floor where the Captain proclaims: 'I'm telling you Joxer . . . th' whole world's . . . in a terrible state o' . . . chassis.'

The comic scenes in this play are underscored with bitter disillusion. The ironic juxtapositions of the humorous and the tragic are so skilfully balanced that there is no descent to bathos and melodrama. Juno, the mother, is one of the greatest creations in drama. In her brave and hopeless struggle against disaster, she is as indomitable as another mother, Maurya in *Riders to the Sea*.

O'Casey's *The Plough and the Stars* was produced at the Abbey in 1926. Again the setting is in the Dublin slums but the period is during the Insurrection, Easter Week, 1916. The seizure of the Post Office, the declaration of an Irish Republic, the short but bloody battle in different parts of Dublin, and the arrest and execution of the leaders is now a matter of history. O'Casey portrays how the tenement-dwellers and some British Tommies reacted to this fateful week in the history of English-Irish relations. In the first act we are introduced to a wider cross-section of slum-dwellers than in the earlier plays: Nora Clitheroe, a young and attractive newly wed, and her husband Jack Clitheroe who has just been promoted in the ranks of the

Irish Citizen Army; the Young Covey, a socialist; Uncle Peter, an ineffective old crank, a member of the Irish National Foresters; Fluther Good, a hard-drinking handyman; Bessie Burgess, a true-blue loyalist whose son is fighting with the British in France; Mrs. Gogan, a dawny little woman who has a passion for funerals, and her consumptive daughter, Mollser.

The second act is set in a public-house where we meet Rosie Redmond, a prostitute, who chats with Fluther, the Covey and the others while an orator addresses a political meeting outside. The words are excerpts from an oration by P. H. Pearse, one of the leaders of Easter Week: 'It is a glorious thing to see arms in the hands of Irishmen. We must accustom ourselves to the thought of arms. . . . Bloodshed is a cleansing and sanctifying thing and the nation that regards it as the final horror has lost its manhood. . . . There are many things more horrible than bloodshed, and slavery is one of them.'

Rosie complains about a lack of business since all the men are 'thinkin' of higher things than girl's garthers'; the Young Covey will have none of the brand of freedom preached as it does not conform to 'Generski's thesis on the origin, evolution and development of the proletariat'; Bessie Burgess has 'a storm of anger in her heart at everybody's disregard of the poor Tommies at the front who had gone to fight for "poor little Catholic Belgium" '; while Fluther and Uncle Peter enjoy their 'balls of malt' until the whiskey and the oratory makes the blood boil in their Irish veins. Only Jack Clitheroe joins the fighting men and throws aside his distracted wife Nora. She searches for Jack through the bullet-riddled streets but even when she finds him, he is 'afraid to say that he is afraid'. But Nora's dilemma, Mollser's illness, and the squabbles between Uncle Peter and the Covey, and between Bessie Burgess and Mrs. Gogan, are all forgotten when word comes that some of the shops in O'Connell Street are wide open to looters. And this time an army marches forth from the tenement to pick up 'anything which has gone astray in the general confusion of battle'. They bring home the loot in prams and the whiskey in large jars. In the last act, tragedy closes in. They are trapped in an upper room with a red sky visible through the window from the blazing buildings. In the middle of the room there is a coffin in which little consumptive Mollser lies dead. Nora has lost her mind and has no one to care for her but Bessie. Fluther and the men play cards while the fighting comes closer. Bessie is shot by a sniper while trying to save Nora from going in search of her Jack who has been killed in action. The men are taken away by the British Tommies a few of whom remain behind to drink a cup of tea and sing 'Keep the Home Fires Burning'.

In this great last act, the tentative pacifism and socialism of O'Casey becomes explicit. In this and in the earlier plays he portrays the viewpoints of many factions and many individuals with masterly detachment and compassion. His language is a synthesis of the Dublin vernacular, Shakespeare and the King James version of the Bible. In the longer speeches, one detects the rhythms of Synge's poetic prose. The voice is the voice of Dublin but, time and again, the dialogue has the colour, exuberance and the dying fall of some of the great speeches in Synge's plays. O'Casey does not romanticise his characters but against a background of the Irish revolution, he portrays the courage of women and the cowardice of men when faced with a tragedy which overwhelms them. But the cowards are gay and human, and the brave only crave a home or a husband.

In Dublin, nowadays, praise of O'Casey's early Abbey plays seems irrelevant and impertinent. As Brendan Behan once remarked it is 'like praising the Lakes of Killarney'. But this was not always the case. O'Casey remained ever conscious of the fact that when these fine plays were first produced, many of his fellow-writers and some critics were, to say the least, rather disparaging of his great achievement. Everyone has his own favourite among the early plays. Today *The Plough and the Stars* holds the record as far as popularity with audiences goes. It had the advantage that on its first production in 1926, it was heralded by that recipe for box-office success, an Abbey row.

During the fourth performance, the stage was invaded by an organised group who considered the carrying of the National flag into a public-house, in the second act, a public insult to the insurgents of Easter Week, especially when one of the onlookers was a prostitute. Fighting broke out between the cast and some of the invaders. The latter, however, had little or no support and the public protest was not repeated. The controversy continued in the press and in debating societies.

The juxtaposition of tragedy and comedy, of prayer and mockery, of heroism and ridicule, often in the same scene, must have come as a shock to those early audiences who were unaccustomed to the genius of O'Casey who could handle the stuff of melodrama with ironic detachment. Even more so than in *Juno and the Paycock* and *The Shadow of a Gunman*, there is a perfect equilibrium between the comic and tragic elements in *The Plough and the Stars*. Apart from the merits of the individual plays, the trio remains an incomparable portrayal of Ireland in revolution.

After the great success of *The Plough and the Stars*, O'Casey went to live in London where he married a musical comedy actress of Irish birth, Eileen Reynolds. Most Dublin theatre-goers, despite the protests and the disparagement of his works in literary circles, would have liked him to continue to write in his old vein as an ironic observer of Irish failings and hypocrisies. He left behind his Dublin subjects to tackle a play on the First World War which he entitled *The Silver Tassie*. It was a partial breakaway from his Abbey successes. The first act is set in Dublin and is realistic in approach. The second expressionistic act takes place near the battlefront in France. There are later scenes in a hospital ward and in a football clubhouse which are Irish and realistic. Although the main characters are Dubliners, neither their working-class background nor their Irishness is strongly stressed. Irish politics are ignored and the play as a whole can be read as a protest against the brutality and stupidity of war, any war. In the first act, Harry Heegan a soldier home on furlough has won the Silver Tassie for the local football club. There is a celebration with his club-mates;

but the wives and mothers are afraid that the boys may miss the boat which will take them back to France and the battlefront and so lose the separation allowances.

The second act opens in a 'lacerated ruin of what was once a monastery' and in a series of short expressionistic scenes, we meet soldiers, officers, stretcher-bearers, and war-office officials. They intone and chant in the manner of the expressionist drama of George Kaiser and Ernst Toller. The soldiers pray not before a crucifix but to a big howitzer gun. When staged effectively, this fantastic scene rivets the attention of the audience with its nightmarish quality of something half-seen and half-understood.

The footballer Harry is a crippled hero in the third act. He loses his girl to a pal. In the last act Harry is back at the football club in a wheel-chair and he tastes gall when offered a drink from the Silver Tassie.

Irish interest in *The Silver Tassie* has centred not on this burningly sincere if lop-sided anti-war play but on the controversy which arose from its rejection by the Abbey in 1928. The verbal battle between Yeats and O'Casey provided more drama than the play itself. Some newspapers published the correspondence between the two writers in dialogue form; others reported that O'Casey had challenged Yeats to a duel. In giving his reasons for the rejection, Yeats had written to O'Casey:

There is no dominating action: neither psychological unity nor unity of action. Your great power in the past has been the creation of some unique character who dominated all about him and was himself a main impulse in some action that filled the play from beginning to end. The mere greatness of the World War has thwarted you, it has refused to become a mere background, and obtrudes itself upon the stage as so much deadwood that will not burn in the dramatic fire.

Dramatic action is a fire that must burn up everything but itself; there should be no room in a play for anything that does not belong to it; the whole history of the world must be reduced to wallpaper in front of which the characters must pose and speak. Among the things that dramatic action must burn up are the author's opinions; while he is writing he has no business to know anything that is not a portion of the action.[1]

O'Casey, infuriated by Yeats's mandarin prose, replied:

I have pondered in my heart your expression that 'the history of the world must be reduced to wallpaper' and I can find in it only the pretentious bigness of a pretentious phrase. I thank you, out of more politeness; but I must refuse even to try to do it. This is exactly, in my opinion (there goes a cursed opinion again), what most of the Abbey dramatists are trying to do—building up, building up little worlds of wallpaper, and hiding striding life behind it all. Your statements about 'psychological unity, unity of action etc.' . . . are to me glib, glib, ghosts. It seems to me they were created, and will continue to be spoken for ever and ever, by professors in schools for the propagation of drama. (I have held these infants in my arms a thousand times and they are all the same—fat, lifeless, wrinkled things that give one a pain in his belly looking at them.)[2]

Controversy apart, the rejection upset O'Casey's confidence in his capacity to handle a large theme in an unconventional dramatic form. A London production by the Charles B. Cochran Management, with Charles Laughton playing Harry Heegan, and a magnificent battlefront set by Augustus John was acclaimed by the critics as exciting theatre but they were divided on its merits as a play. A belated production at the Abbey in 1935 gave rise to another controversy in which O'Casey was accused of parodying religious ritual in the expressionistic second act. An Abbey director and playwright, Brinsley Macnamara, resigned in protest against what he considered the anti-Catholic sentiments in the play, alleging that he had been out-voted by his fellow-directors when he proposed the cutting of certain passages. The Catholic Press were loud in their denunciations. O'Casey, on the other hand, saw jealousy and intrigue where there was nothing more than plain

[1] *The Irish Statesman*, 9 June 1928.
[2] *Ibid.*

stupidity. Gabriel Fallon comments fairly in *Sean O'Casey: The Man I Knew*:

> Most of this lack of understanding was due to a hopelessly retarded Catholic intellectuality. In his defence against indecency O'Casey, quoted *inter alia* the words 'bastards', 'son-of-a-bitch' and 'arse' used in Paul Claudel's *The Silver Slipper* translated from the French by Father John O'Connor. But this would hardly convince people who cherish a Catholic literature that is wholly narrow and sectarian instead of fully and universally Christian, or as Romano Guerdini puts it, one embracing 'the whole world spiritually as a vast Kingdom of unrealities'. Such people as Mr. O'Casey's opponents in this issue have never hesitated to resort to ways unspiritual and rude and dubiously Catholic to uphold, as they believe, the name and dignity of the Church. It is a tribute to the salutary effect of *The Silver Tassie* that its Dublin audiences did not riot'.[3]

Not only did audiences not riot but Hugh Hunt's Abbey production in 1972 has been generally acclaimed by critics and public. With the advantages of hindsight, it is now easy to deplore the Abbey's original decision to reject *The Silver Tassie*. Even if one accepts all that Yeats wrote by way of criticism, the Abbey board should have realised that O'Casey was entitled to a production of what they regarded as a disappointing play. The final decision might well have been left to the audience who had been so right about his plays in the past. The directors, a few years earlier, had accepted O'Casey's *Nannie's Night Out*, not as the work of an apprentice writer but as the fourth play of an established playwright. It was a curiously muddled piece about a young 'spunker', a red-biddy drinker, Irish Nannie, who drops dead in a shop where the customers indulge in horseplay and poor jokes. It was a dismal flop, but O'Casey manfully abided by the verdict and later dismissed the play as 'rather negligible'.

It is worth recalling that the ordinary public and the theatregoers in Dublin were on O'Casey's side from the beginning. They flocked to his plays whenever they were given an opportunity to do so. O'Casey never again submitted a play of his to

[3] Gabriel Fallon, *Sean O Casey: The Man I Knew*, 1965, p. 133.

the Abbey. For a period in the 1950s as a result of a quarrel with the Dublin Theatre Festival Committee, he prohibited professional productions of any of his plays in the Republic. None the less, Irish playgoers treated him as the great celebrity he was and gave him as much recognition as any living writer should expect in his native land. This should have pleased him greatly, as the fountainhead of O'Casey's creative impulse was Ireland and her people. There were many in Dublin who were inclined to belittle and berate him whenever he failed to fit in with preconceived notions of how a great writer should behave. And being a vain man, a proud man, he in turn berated his critics for their shortcomings.

But the greater justification was on his side. For many outstanding artists are critical, often savagely critical of the follies and failings and even of some of the virtues of their countrymen. O'Casey with his searing sincerity and his passionate concern for social justice was no exception. And in remaining true to himself it is little wonder that he seemed to be false to others at times.

Great dramatist as he was, he lacked intellectual calm as a writer. In the heat of his struggle against pain and poverty he often lashed out at friend and foe alike. He could not, for example, praise his lifelong hero, Jim Larkin, without seeming to disparage James Connolly, the most vital social thinker of that generation. A great deal of his polemical writing serves to emphasise the Protestantism of Sean O'Casey. He protested. He was a Protestant in the way that Dean Swift was a Protestant. Indeed, the downfall of Parnell, Ireland's last great Protestant leader left a wound in O'Casey's mind that time could not heal.

Some of the literary judgements in his semi-autobiographical books are wayward when not downright unfair. Moreover, in these six volumes, the dramatist assiduously presents an image of himself as a slum-dweller in the most deprived sense of the word. This is something less than the whole truth. Nor is it a fact that he grew up in relative ignorance and was largely self-educated. In later years he certainly suffered poverty through illness and unemployment but it is difficult to understand how, with his background and above-average opportunities, he was unable to get a better job than that of a labourer. There is some evidence of pilfering from his employers while in his teens but this is unimportant like Shakespeare's deer stealing. Brendan Behan once said that he was brought up among people 'who would lift anything that wasn't nailed down'. But Brendan, although often broke, never kept up the pretence of being poor. Like Oscar Wilde, his standard of destitution was pretty high.

But in any search for biographical facts, there is the danger that the genius of O'Casey the dramatist—and he remained a dramatist even in the autobiographies—may be obscured by an approach which pays due attention to everything but the plays themselves. Some non-Irish admirers of O'Casey have spent much time and energy in an attempt to identify the prototypes of many of O'Casey's characters. Such critical methods are about as rewarding as 'chasing butterflies in Knocksedan'. For example, it is interesting to know that Micheál Ó Maoláin as Arainn was O'Casey's room-mate in 1920 at 35 Mountjoy Square, when they both experienced a Black and Tan raid which is echoed in *The Shadow of a Gunman*. Micheál Ó Maoláin has revealed this himself in an article in Irish in the May 1955 issue of *Feasta*. Neighbours had suspected that O'Casey was a gunman but, according to Ó Maoláin, he remained silent and frightened during the actual raid. There the resemblance between O'Casey—Ó Maoláin and Davoren—Shields of *The Shadow of a Gunman* ends. All who knew Micheál Ó Maoláin as a dedicated worker for Trade Unionism and the Irish Language in Coisde na bPáistí, will find it hard to identify him with the comic and cowardly pedlar Seamus Shields in *The Shadow of a Gunman*—a scamp on the grand scale, as Ivor Brown so aptly describes him. But Saros Cowasjee, David Krause and R. M. Fox who should have known better, give currency to the fable.

There may be something of Micheál Ó Maoláin in several O'Casey characters; for a dramatist takes hints from life, but he transmutes his materials into characters who are essentially his own. The same select creativity is at work in the somewhat idealised portrait of Sean Casside of the *soi-disant* autobiographies. One does not turn to these for a literal presentation of fact. Passion and bitterness have distorted O'Casey's vision of Sean. But his folly was his own, and one cannot but admire his unflinching defiance, a not uncommon characteristic of the wilder forms of genius. Nor is it necessary to take O'Casey's self-avowed communism for granted. Even a modern Marxist or Maoist would find this great poetic-humanist a strange bedfellow.

Only in one of O'Casey's later plays on Irish subjects does he toe the party line. In *The Star Turns Red* dedicated 'to the men and women who fought through the great Dublin lockout in nineteen hundred and thirteen', he abandons the socialist/pacifist approach of *The Silver Tassie* and the earlier plays. He now accepts that social revolution must bring sacrifice, even if it means the death of thousands as a necessary step towards a Marxist goal. When it was published in 1940, even George Jean Nathan, a life-long admirer of O'Casey, conceded that 'Communism, one fears, has now adversely affected Sean O'Casey as a dramatic artist'. Stephen Spender was also of the opinion that O'Casey's zeal for party-line propaganda had perverted his artistic vision.

It is interesting to note that three years later, in *Red Roses for Me*, he reverted to the more human aspects of the social struggle. Again he draws largely on his experiences in Dublin during the Transport Workers' Strike in 1913. The hero, Ayamonn, who saw a shilling rise in pay 'in the shape of a new world' is, to a large extent, a personification or idealisation of the younger O'Casey. Ayamonn is a young Protestant worker, a lover of Shakespeare and an active trades unionist who is in love with a Catholic girl. He is thus embroiled in sectarian conflict both as a lover and a worker. He accepts struggle, sacrifice and death in his altruistic desire to see a better life for the common man. His beloved Shiela, after Ayamonn's death, becomes petty and self-centred. Here we have the obverse of the O'Casey coin, in contrast to the early O'Casey plays where the women were brave and the men wastrels. Generally, he seems to take a critical or derisive view of all working-class men, in spite of his championship of Dublin workers as a whole. Every man's ideas and ideals are muddled and unreal; not a man would stick to his guns. He was quite different where women were concerned. Perhaps he was not capable of being fair to his own sex. There are some delightfully comic creations in *Red Roses for Me* like 'Brennan on the Moor'. The third act, set by the Liffey quays, presents an apocalyptic vision of a new and beautiful Dublin that the younger O'Casey imagined in his dreams. The populace chant—

> We swear to release thee from hunger and hardship
> From things that are ugly and common and mean.
> The people together shall build a great city
> The finest and fairest that ever was seen.

A contemporary critic rightly commented that 'the O'Casey who clutched in dementia at schoolboy communism in *The Star Turns Red* has now passed on to the Apotheosis of Man, after the manner of Shelley, in *Red Roses for Me*'.

O'Casey brought to the Abbey stage characters as vivid and voluble as the country people of Synge, Colum and T. C. Murray but he portrayed them against a background of city tenements in post-revolutionary Ireland. New aspects of life in provincial towns were revealed in the plays of Lennox Robinson and Brinsley Macnamara. The latter's *Look at the Heffernans* already has some of the old-world charm of a period comedy. In contrast, his sombre tragedy, *Margaret Gillan*, enveloped in a Strindbergian gloom, is something of a flawed masterpiece. It awaits a native Ingmar Bergman to direct an actress of exceptional range in the name-part.

The late 1920s saw the renewal of opposition to the peasant play. There is an interesting entry in Lady Gregory's Journals under the date 24 May 1926: 'On one of his last days, Yeats seeing me writing asked what I was working at, I said "A Play, but I mustn't mention it to you, because it is a peasant play. It is on the index!" For he (Yeats) had been saying that "Dublin won't stand for any more peasant work".'[4] What Dublin would or would not stand for was of little concern to Yeats! But there was a climate of opinion which regarded the peasant play as a thing of the past in the new and more bourgeois Ireland which took shape at the beginning of the 1930s. It was felt that there was little place in the theatre for plays without a measure of international significance. None of the Abbey dramatists succeeded very well in their portrayals of middle-class life. O'Casey's later plays such as *The Bishop's Bonfire* and *Cock-a-Doodle Dandy* in which he discards the realistic treatment of slum life and aims at a partly symbolic and stylised approach have met with little success so far. He awaits, like Yeats, a producer of genius who will weld together such disparate elements as dance, music and speech. Lennox Robinson who seemed better equipped than most to write a suburban or bourgeois drama of a realistic kind, achieved less than his best in *The Round Table*, *Portrait* and *The White Blackbird*. He often portrays the countryman townified or citified, but beneath the urban veneer and the superficial gloss we see his characters unmistakably for what they are—peasants in aspic.

In the late 1920s Denis Johnston, working mainly under the influence of German expressionism, tried to give Irish playwriting a new slant in which he was greatly helped by the excellent presentation and style of the Dublin Gate Theatre which had been founded by Hilton Edwards and Micheál MacLiammóir. This exciting and brilliant theatrical venture was to become the most stimulating and vital force in the Irish theatre in the 1930s.

[4] Lennox Robinson (ed.), *Lady Gregory's Journals*, n.d., pp. 263–4.

CHAPTER NINE

The Gate Theatre and Some Actors

When Hilton Edwards and Micheál MacLiammóir decided to start a theatre, there seemed to be no good reason why they should choose Dublin. Previous attempts to launch an art theatre for the production of world masterpieces and plays of international repute had not been encouraging. Although they both had received their first training in the English theatre, their backgrounds were different.

Hilton Edwards, an Englishman, had played with Charles Doran's Shakespearean Company before he joined the Old Vic. Micheál MacLiammóir, born in Cork, had been an actor since childhood having played with Sir Herbert Beerbohm Tree. After he had studied art at the Slade School, he spent some years on the Continent before he returned to Ireland where he became known as an artist and writer in Irish. He had painted sets for Edward Martyn's Irish Theatre and played there at least once. In 1927, he joined the Shakespearean Company of his brother-in-law, Anew McMaster, for a tour of the Irish provinces.

Anew McMaster was one of the most remarkable actors ever to tour in Ireland. Particularly in rural Ireland, he was held in that kind of reverential awe that old-timers reserved for Barry Sullivan. He was the last of the actor-managers on the Irish stage and played in the grand manner of an older tradition. He played Shakespeare in villages so remote that some of the locals believed that he not only acted in the plays but that he wrote them also. No Irish actor had been so generous with his talent. His performance as Othello was superb by any standard. He gave their initial start and training to two or three generations of actors. It was while playing in McMaster's Company that Hilton Edwards met Micheál MacLiammóir. The latter, in *Theatre in Ireland,* pays tribute to McMaster's influence on the theatre particularly in the provinces:

> In the middle of the 20's, with O'Casey as undisputed ruler of the day at the Abbey; with Robinson at work on that series of tribeless and nationless comedies which reflected more of the restless decade's fashion than of himself; with Yeats in the throes of his plays for dancers, and with the country itself emerging, with a certain bitter gaiety, from the ardours of civil war—to be precise in the summer of 1925—a young actor of Irish birth, Anew McMaster, decided, in the middle of a vastly varied career, to tour with a repertoire of classic plays, mainly Shakespearean, to be presented, not in Dublin, but in the country towns of Ireland. It was a bold and unexpected move, for the places destined for the experience had known little hitherto but popular dramas and comedies imported mostly from London long since and played by such companies as Dobell's, Carrickfords, O'Brien and Ireland's and others. These included in their programmes favourites as deeply dyed and tried as *Shall We Forgive Her, East Lynne, The Lights of London, The Bad Girl of the Family* and *Charley's Aunt,* and towns like Cahirciveen or Ballinasloe or Athlone were considered unsuitable for more austere ventures. But McMaster, an odd sort of man, thought otherwise and his productions of *Hamlet, Othello* and *Macbeth* after a few months of uneven and occasionally disastrous business, began to attract a surprising public. Shakespeare, and later Sheridan and Goldsmith, became the fashion of the country towns, and there is a story famous in, I think, the County of Clare, of how, when some modern comedy was announced for Saturday night, an old man standing at the back of the pit shouted out that they of the town were 'too backwardy for them highbrow shows, and what about giving us *Julius Caesar*?'

> McMaster certainly had done much for the taste of country audiences, though there was nothing about his programme that even remotely reflected or revealed the national life, and although at later dates he appeared for successful seasons at the Abbey in Dublin

with such famous artists as Mrs. Patrick Campbell, Sir Frank Benson and others, his real business in Ireland was and still is with those townspeople who formed for him a public that was in many ways nearer, in the alertness of their ear and the purity of their speech, to that of Shakespeare's own day than are the jaded spectators of the big theatres, who endure the long Elizabethan periods mainly in order to find out how some fashionable player or producer will handle them. It is certain too that McMaster's influence on the amateur players of these towns has been as considerable in its way as the influence of the Abbey playwrights who provide for them most of their material, and the amateur movement cannot be overlooked in the dramatic history of any country as new to the theatre as Ireland or as sparse in population, for where but among these can players or public, isolated from the life of the big cities, receive their first experience?[1]

After McMaster's death, in 1962, Harold Pinter who had toured Ireland with the McMaster Company under the name David Baron, wrote an appreciative memoir of the prowess and magnetism of the last of the great touring actor-managers.

MacLiammóir had written a play, *Diarmuid agus Gráinne*, in Irish and a translation was billed for production by McMaster's Company in Kilkenny. There was a last-minute change of plans and Edwards and MacLiammóir came to Dublin to hire a hall for the production of the play. There they met Madame Bannard Cogley and Gearóid O Lochlainn who also were in search of a theatre at the time. Eventually, they leased the small Peacock Theatre, which had been built by the Abbey Board as an experimental annexe to the Abbey itself.

The first production of the Dublin Gate Theatre—named after Peter Godfrey's London Theatre—was on 14 October 1928 when Ibsen's *Peer Gynt* was staged in the Peacock. During their first two seasons, the sixteen plays staged conformed in the main to the avowed policy—the presentation of plays of unusual interest, and experimentation in methods of presentation freed from the conventionalities of commercial theatre. It was only in Dublin, of course, that John Galsworthy's *The*

[1] Micheál MacLiammóir, *Theatre in Ireland*, 1964, pp. 21–3.

Little Man or David Sears *Juggernaut* could qualify as 'unusual'. The last-named was an Abbey reject and there certainly was nothing unusual about that. What was unusual was that the most remarkable play the Gate ever presented was a play which had been submitted to the Abbey but which the directors felt required a style of production outside the range of the Abbey producer at the time. It was returned to the author but the Abbey gave a small subsidy to the Gate Company to enable them to produce it in the Peacock. The play was *The Old Lady Says 'No'* by Denis Johnston.

Denis Johnston was born in Dublin in 1901. Following in his father's footsteps he was called to the Bar but for most of his life, he has been a playwright, war-correspondent, broadcaster and lecturer. The very title of his first play *The Old Lady Says 'No'* has been the subject of rumour. Dublin legend has it that 'The Old Lady' of the title was Lady Gregory and that she was responsible for the alleged 'rejection' by the Abbey. As a reading of the text reveals, 'The Old Lady' is none other than Ireland, Cathleen Ní Houlihan herself, who, as the author shows, can be a bit of a bitch at times. The grant of a small subsidy by the Abbey for the production of this play by another company was, in a way, an admission of failure on the part of the Abbey directors. Here was a new and exciting young playwright ready to break with tradition, and the National Theatre was not able to mount a production. The sheer brilliance of Denis Johnston's first dramatic experiment was a challenge to the resourcefulness of producer and cast.

The first scene takes place at the Priory, Rathfarnham, where Ireland's most popular revolutionary hero, Robert Emmet, and his beloved, Sarah Curran, are declaiming romantic verse which is a skilful medley of quotations from anthologies of the nineteenth century. Major Sirr and his redcoats arrive to arrest Emmet who strikes a stance appropriate to an Irish martyr. He is grounded by a blow of a rifle. Then the audience senses that something has gone wrong—it appears that the actor playing Emmet has been accidentally injured by the stage blow. There is some confusion as the producer comes before the curtain to ask if there is a doctor in the house. A doctor goes to the assistance of the actor and it is only when there is a change of lighting to suggest a new scene that the audience realise that they have been taken in. Although reminiscent of Pirandello's *Henry IV*, this opening is a brilliant *coup-de-théâtre*.

The rest of the play takes place in the mind of the actor playing Robert Emmet. The play within the play is in marked contrast to the romantic opening scene. The actor playing Emmet imagines himself foot-loose in modern Dublin in search of Rathfarnham and his beloved Sarah. The satire is directed not against the Emmet of history but against the romanticised hero of poetry and song who is always brave and always defeated. The incongruity between the outworn romanticism of the past and the work-a-day reality of modern Dublin is theatrically effective. The author, with disarming candour, has left it on record that he scarcely wrote a line of dialogue which, in the main, consists of sayings and quotations culled from the sages and cynics, poltroons and poets who have graced the Irish scene. Indeed, the wealth of allusion presupposes a considerable knowledge of Irish history and literature. The play's effectiveness is limited to the extent that its excellence can only be sampled in performance. It has been rightly pointed out by its original producer, Hilton Edwards, that the text reads like a railway-guide and plays like Tristan and Isolde. None the less it is not only one of the best first plays ever written for the Irish theatre but perhaps the only work in the expressionistic mode of the twenties still of interest today.

Denis Johnston's next play, *The Moon in the Yellow River*, is more realistic and conventional. Perhaps, for this reason, it was readily accepted by the Abbey where it was first produced in 1931 and frequently revived. The plot revolves around a plot to blow up a power station which is manned by a German engineer. Some Irish revolutionaries led by one Darrell Blake plan to blow up the power house with a special type of shell which has been invented by two crazy inventors. A ruthless Free State Officer, Lanigan, however, shoots Blake but the power-house is destroyed by accident. There are several subplots which involve comic characters who add light relief to the solemn arguments about machines versus men, and German efficiency versus Irish fecklessness. There is much effective satire but one senses that it is directed against too-easy targets.

Another Abbey play, *Blind Man's Buff*, was originally billed as by Ernst Toller and Denis Johnston. Whatever its indebtedness to Toller's *The Blind Goddess*, which does not appear to be great, it remains the best play about a murder trial yet seen in Dublin. A doctor on trial for having poisoned his wife disregards his Counsel's advice and attacks the character of a witness for the prosecution. He then lays himself open to cross-examination on character and the disclosure that he performed an illegal operation on his mistress, which provides the necessary motive for the alleged murder of his wife. The court-room scenes are excellent, with sharp characterisations of the Irish legal profession, and there is a surprise denouement. Another forensic piece, *Strange Occurrence on Ireland's Eye*, on the well-known trial of an artist Kirwan for the murder of his wife, proved less successful.

Two of his earlier works staged at the Gate, *A Bride for the Unicorn* and *Storm Song*, have shared the fate of most of the post-expressionistic plays of the early 1930s—that of museum pieces. A nineteen-sixteen play, *The Scythe and the Sunset*, lacks the emotional impact of *The Plough and the Stars*, but shows Johnston as an intelligent and dispassionate observer of the Irish scene. His Swift play, *The Dreaming Dust*, is very much an intellectual exercise based on his theory of Swift's relationship with Stella which he dealt with at length in a later book on the subject.

In the early 1930s, through the generosity of Edward Pakenham, 6th Earl of Longford, a playwright and a distinguished patron of the arts, it was made possible for the Gate Company to continue their work in a 400-seat theatre in the Rotunda Buildings where for the next decade they staged a varied repertoire with a professionalism in presentation that has had a lasting effect on the standards of Irish theatre.

Although plays by T. C. Murray, Robert Collis, Christine Longford, Mary Manning, Lord Longford and Micheál

MacLiammóir were staged from time to time, the Gate Theatre failed to attract a steady succession of new playwrights and eventually became a valuable showcase for the classics and international drama, rather than a creative force as far as playwriting is concerned. Lord Longford, who later formed his own company, was even more committed to the classics of the Elizabethan and Restoration theatre. Notable exceptions were Lord and Lady Longford's adaptations of Sheridan Le Fanu's weird stories as well as their original plays.

During the war years, the Edwards–MacLiammóir Company moved across the river to the larger Gaiety Theatre. The economics of a large commercial theatre compelled them to adjust their sights and stage Broadway and West End successes, and 'plays of the film' such as *Rebecca*. MacLiammóir, in his book *Theatre in Ireland*, refers a little sadly to:

the growing taste for the West End and Broadway commercial success, never in the English language to be done quite as well by Irish actors as the British or American ones, so that in the moment of their performance or the enjoyment of their results there is always the dull conscience stricken pang, that one is doing, or reaping the benefit of, a slightly second rate thing; a thing which one knows can be and has been done more perfectly elsewhere.[2]

It is now part of theatrical history that Orson Welles and James Mason played at the Gate for a few seasons. But the performance of the decade was the Hamlet of Micheál MacLiammóir. There have been many Irish Hamlets since the play was first staged in the Smock Alley Theatre in the late 1670s. The prompt-books of that theatre confirm this, but neither the exact date nor the name of the leading player is now ascertainable. Robert Wilks, Spranger Barry, Thomas Sheridan and Henry Mossop played this part later, but they were more highly regarded in other Shakespearean parts.

In the nineteenth century, the Dublin actor, Gustavus Vaughan Brooke first played Hamlet when he was only twenty-four years of age. After him came Barry Sullivan whose statue

[2] Micheál MacLiammóir, *Theatre in Ireland*, 1964, pp. 31–2.

as Hamlet can be seen in Glasnevin Cemetery—the only statue of an actor in Ireland. Although proud of his Irish ancestry, Sullivan was born in Birmingham. His prowess as a Shakespearean actor will not be forgotten as long as the dramatic criticism of George Bernard Shaw is read and valued.

To at least two generations of playgoers, the by-no-means-gloomy Dane of Anew McMaster will be familiar. In more recent times, Sir Tyrone Guthrie produced a Hamlet with Ronald Ibbs; and there was a Longford production with Michael Ripper. Cyril Cusack's interpretation of the rôle was certainly the most controversial.

MacLiammóir's Hamlet, first seen in 1932, was unquestionably the greatest creation of this brilliant actor's career. 'The outstanding quality of his Hamlet was his youth,' wrote a contemporary critic, 'youth lonely and outraged, and the interest in this performance lay in noting how he enriched the tragedy.'[3] It overshadows his plays, which were eminently theatrical, and even his one-man show on Wilde, *The Importance of Being Oscar*, which was a reincarnation.

It is generally accepted that the Abbey actor, F. J. McCormick was the most versatile of Irish performers. His real name was Peter Judge and he was born in Skerries, Co. Dublin, in 1891. He gained his first experience as an amateur while he was a clerk in the Civil Service. Soon he was playing in Queen's Theatre melodramas such as *The Shaughraun* and *Father Murphy*. Fred O'Donovan, then manager of the Abbey, invited him to join the company with whom he made his first appearance in 1918. Between then and his death in 1947, he played nearly four hundred parts in the Abbey. These included Oedipus in the W. B. Yeats version of *Sophocles* and the name part in *King Lear*. His preference was for character comedy and he was always at his best in plays by George Shiels, Brinsley Macnamara and O'Casey. Shortly before his death he played in two films, *Hungry Hill* and *Odd Man Out*, in which he won international acclaim for his performance as Shell. Dublin playgoers are not likely to forget his Seamus Shields in *The Shadow of a*

[3] Bulmer Hobson (ed.), *The Gate Theatre—Dublin*, 1934, p. 41.

Gunman and his Joxer in *Juno and the Paycock*. Of his Joxer, Seán O'Casey was prepared to say that McCormick had created a comic figure even greater than the dramatist's conception of the part.

As an actor-producer, Hilton Edwards in the heyday of the Gate towered over his contemporaries. His influence was most strongly felt as a director in complete control of his production. Lighting, costuming, décor, whether the play was ancient or modern, showed his firm individual style and had the stamp of excellence. Just as the Abbey taught audiences how to use their ears, the Gate accustomed Dubliners to using their eyes as well as their ears. This was indeed a triumph in a country where the visual arts had been neglected and unappreciated. Lennox Robinson, a former Abbey director, has commented on the poor décor of the early Abbey presentations, on the 'incredibly graceless and ugly' costumes, and on 'the green jackets, red caps, trimmed with shells' which Yeats considered suitable for the demons in *The Countess Cathleen*. Charles Rickett's costume designs for *On Baile's Strand* and Gordon Craig's designs for *The Hour Glass* were notable exceptions. It was only after the advent of the Gate that the Abbey employed designers such as Tanya Moseiwitsch, who raised presentation standards. The Gate style was eclectic while that of the Abbey was indigenous. Gate actors because of the extent of their repertoire and the fact that its leading players had considerable and varied professional experience abroad before they came to Dublin, had a wider range of technique. The Abbey, on the other hand, recruited its players mainly from its own School of Acting or from the amateur movement. Only occasionally were professional players from other companies invited to join the company except as guest artists for a special production. The hallmark of an Abbey show was fine teamwork and ensemble playing. The Abbey has been primarily a playwright's theatre in so far as it was writers such as Yeats, Synge and O'Casey rather than the producer/directors who shaped what is widely accepted as the Abbey tradition. The Gate, on the other hand, had a greater influence on décor and production technique.

THE GATE THEATRE AND SOME ACTORS

In the 1940s and 1950s, new groups, usually headed by actors, rose and fell like ninepins. In the mid-1940s the Players Theatre, led by a group of dissenting Abbey actors with the high-minded and short-lived enthusiasm of youth, staged plays by Gerard Healy, Liam Redmond and others. Shelah Richards, a former Abbey actress, formed a company which presented plays by Paul Vincent Carroll and O'Casey. Stanley Illsley and Leo McCabe not only staged many popular successes but sponsored the visits of leading English companies during their period of management in the Olympia. Cyril Cusack formed a company which presented vintage Shaw and one of the most controversial of the later O'Casey plays, *The Bishop's Bonfire*. Later the Globe Theatre headed by Godfrey Quigley, Norman Rodway and Jim Fitzgerald showed a similar enthusiasm but the rewards were not commensurate with the talent expended.

These were the years of the basement theatres, a few of which like the Lantern have miraculously survived. The New Theatre Group, operating with the same policy and only a tenth of the support of the Unity Theatre in London, strove gallantly for a workers' theatre. But the workers showed little interest in polemics, or, if they did, they preferred the drama of the protest march or the mass meeting.

The Pike Theatre, founded by Alan Simpson and Carolyn Swift in a mews off Herbert Street, were the first to stage the work of Samuel Beckett and Brendan Behan in their native city. They certainly rescued *The Quare Fellow* from oblivion and set Brendan Behan on the high road to international success. How the Pike lost a greater share in that success is revealed by Alan Simpson in his book *Beckett and Behan*:

> We set about looking for a larger theatre in which to revive *The Quare Fellow*. This proved impossible because we could not get any of the large theatres in Dublin to give us a letting. It was partly against Brendan himself, whose alcoholic and proletarian background made the more 'respectable' managements feel that there must be something dubious about a play written by such a person, and launched in a garage. In fact, one management gave as the reason that Brendan's brother, once employed by them as gallery

spot operator in their theatre, had been fired for selling the *Daily Worker* to gallery patrons during working hours, and that they wouldn't dream of having a play in their theatre connected with such a family. However, I believe the reason has something to do with the sort of snivelling inferiority complex that even today affects the Irish Establishment class, which for all its 'Patriotism' believes that nothing is good unless it comes from London. Because it was not until *The Quare Fellow* had been successful in Stratford and the West End that the Abbey saw fit to present the play.

Having failed to secure a large-scale Dublin production, we set about trying to interest a London management in the play, but were pipped at the post by Joan Littlewood and Jerry Raffles, her able and fast-moving chief of staff. This caused a falling out between Brendan and ourselves, because we felt resentful at his having given it to Theatre Workshop behind our backs; while he could not see why his play, so highly praised by the Irish critics, should languish in the drawer of a London theatre manager's office instead of bringing him a reasonable financial return. Actually this happens to a lot of plays, an example being *Waiting for Godot*, which was knocked around, the subject of proposition and counter-proposition, for about two years before its 1955 production in the Arts Theatre.[4]

The limited stage resources of the tiny Pike may have helped to create the atmosphere of isolation and claustrophobia so necessary for *The Quare Fellow* as well as contributing to the isolated no-man's-land mood which suited the nonchalant nihilistic humour of *Waiting for Godot*.

'Into the night, go one and all'—Henley's line will serve as an epitaph for the numerous groups who have striven valiantly to contribute to serious theatre without benefit of subsidy. Even the least successful were not just content to try to keep up with the Jonahs who sit and bewail the plight of the Irish theatre. Among those who, as yet, have not given up the strife are Phyllis Ryan's Gemini Productions which have given special prominence to the plays of Hugh Leonard and John B. Keane.

The best news of the early 1970s is the decision by the Irish Government to grant a subsidy to the Gate Theatre where the

[4] Alan Simpson, *Becket and Behan*, 1962, pp. 55–6.

founders, Edwards and MacLiammóir, have re-opened in a season of international plays. The theatre will also be available for six months of the year to other groups sharing the ambitions of the long line of pioneers, since Edward Martyn's day, who attempted to widen the horizons of the Irish theatre.

1. *The Plough and the Stars*, Abbey Theatre production.
From left: Ria Mooney, W. O'Gorman and F. J. McCormick.

2. *Look at the Heffernans!* by Brinsley Macnamara, Abbey Theatre production. W. O'Gorman (left), F. J. McCormick (centre) and M. J. Dolan (right).

3. *The Well of the Saints* by J. M. Synge. Abbey Theatre Production, 1970, by Hugh Hunt. Eamon Kelly as Martin Doul and Kathleen Barrington as Molly Byrne.

4. *Borstal Boy* by Brendan Behan. Abbey Theatre production, by Tomas MacAnna, 1967. Eamon Kelly (left) and Frank Grimes.

5. *The Shaughraun* by Dion Boucicault. Abbey Theatre production, 1967. Cyril Cusack as Conn.

6. Lady Gregory by Gerald Festus Kelly.

7. William Butler Yeats by Sean O'Sullivan.

8. J. M. Synge by J. B. Yeats.

9. Frank Fay by J. B. Yeats.

10. William G. Fay by J. B. Yeats.

11. F. J. McCormick by Sean O'Sullivan.

12. Sara Allgood by Sarah Purser.

13. Maire O'Neill by J. B. Yeats.

15. Hilton Edwards.

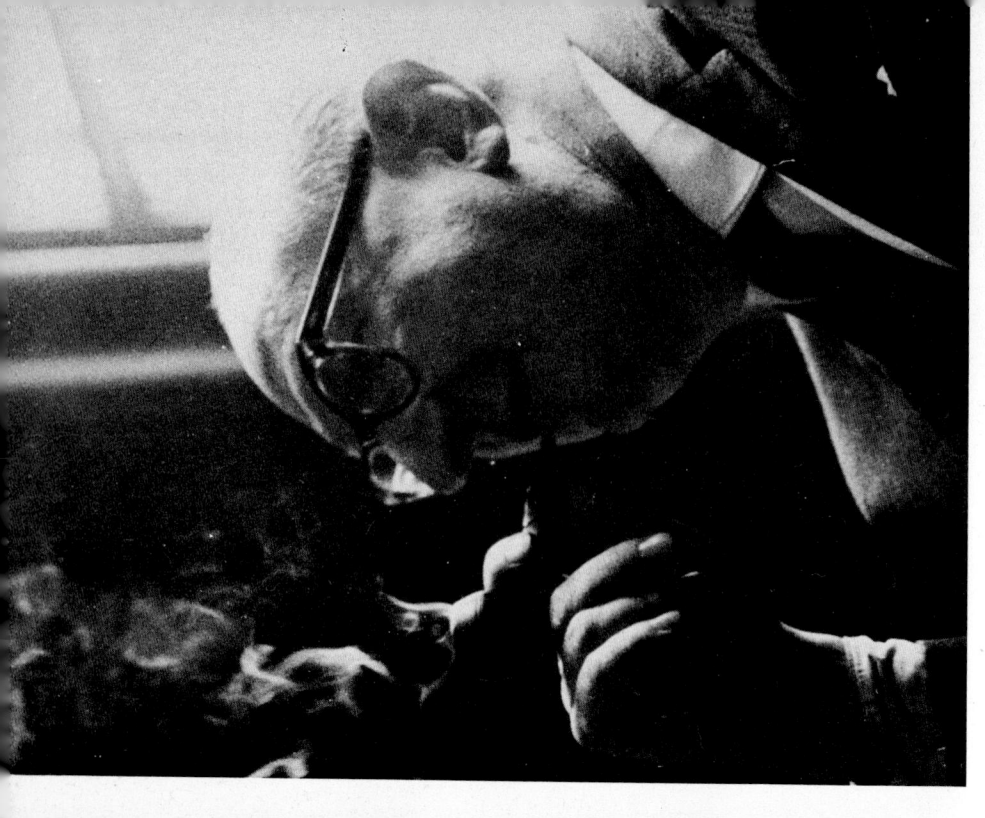

14. Micheal MacLiammoir.

17. The New Abbey Theatre, 1966.

16. The Old Abbey Theatre, 1904-51.

18. Interior of the old Abbey Theatre, from the balcony.
Drawing by Raymond McGrath.

CHAPTER TEN

The End of the Beginning

The most notable Abbey play of the 1930s was Paul Vincent Carroll's *Shadow and Substance*. Many Abbey plays have been labelled anti-clerical; but Carroll, with masterly subtlety, avoids the label by pitting the clergy against themselves. The austere and fastidious Hispanophile, Canon Skerritt is opposed by his two bacon and cabbage curates, his rebellious national teacher and oafish parishioners. His only friend is Brigid, a simple servant girl whose visions of Saint Brigid he neither condones nor pretends to misunderstand; but the Canon's pride and the schoolmaster's insensitivity are the rocks between which the visionary Brigid is crushed. The sad irony is that the hale and hearty curates emerge as the popular heroes.

Some of Carroll's other plays are variations on this theme which he had handled so subtly in *Shadow and Substance*. George Nathan has written enthusiastically of *The White Steed* but it lacks the inner conviction and strength of its prototype. Here was another instance of an Abbey dramatist who, after a brilliant start, failed to stay the course.

After the death of Lady Gregory in 1932, several women dramatists vied for a place in the sun. The most interesting was Teresa Deevy who, in her one-acter, *The King of Spain's Daughter*, and in her full-length *Katie Roche*, wrote sensitively of wilful and romantic young girls who try to come to grips with the workaday realities of a man's world.

THE END OF THE BEGINNING

The Abbey's troubles in the late 1930s and early 1940s have been entertainingly and mischievously related by a former director, Frank O'Connor, in his autobiography and reminiscences:

The New Abbey Policy of competing with Edwards and MacLiammóir I disagreed with on two grounds. One was that it seemed to require two producers when we couldn't afford one. The other and more important reason was that, in my view, it was wrong. For years the directors had been unable to find new Irish plays, or so they said, or so Robinson had persuaded them, and later, when really interesting new plays were submitted, the Board had practically decided beforehand that the plays could be no good. Even when it was working at full capacity the theatre never managed to produce more than a half-dozen new plays a year. I felt that this could be increased to nine or ten, but, allowing for the fact that some of them would have to be popular plays by established playwrights like Robinson himself, Shields (sic) and MacNamara, the production of four or five European classics like *Coriolanus* and *Dr. Faustus* would mean that there would be no opportunity for young serious dramatists. This would mean the end of the literary movement, for magazine and book publishers we had none.

As for the European classics, I had seen them performed as well as I was ever to do and had decided that they might not be as classical as they were generally supposed to be. Shakespeare could be boring, so could Sheridan; one could even get too much of Ibsen and Chekhov. I had not yet classified them as 'Museum Theatre', and in those days would probably have disputed the theory. The theory I later evolved to explain my own disillusionment I have expounded so often that I have almost ceased to believe in it myself. It seemed to me that the theatre is by its nature a contemporary art, a collaboration between author, players and audience, and once the collaboration is broken down by time it cannot be repeated.

There are exceptions, of course, particularly when an old text is rehandled by a modern writer and the staging re-created in terms of a contemporary society. Even with *Hamlet* one can still enable the audience to walk on the razor's edge of real drama, but in my experience it was much easier to make them walk it with some little play by a contemporary author in a local setting. The lightest of Robinson's own comedies had an immediacy of effect that Goethe's

Faust or Ibsen's *Peer Gynt* at the rival theatre did not have. If I was to work for it, the Abbey had to be an all-Irish theatre.

Yeats, too, of course, wanted a living theatre. If he had been younger and in better health he would have come to the theatre himself and insisted on it. It was he who in the middle of the New Abbey Policy was desperately holding on to Lennox Robinson and a few rough and ready comedies, so that when he died he might transmit some part of what he and his friends had achieved in the creation of an original repertory and an original style of acting'.[1]

O'Connor, a short-story writer of genius and a brilliant man-of-letters, had written two successful plays, *The Invincibles* and *In the Train*, in collaboration with the Abbey producer, Hugh Hunt. But after Hunt left the Abbey, O'Connor's subsequent plays were failures and one play, later produced under the title *The Statue's Daughter* at the Gate, had been rejected by his fellow-directors. Never a man to accept decisions by consensus, O'Connor, believing that the mantle of Yeats enwrapped him, quarrelled with his fellow-directors, including his first friend in Dublin, Lennox Robinson. A Dublin wit remarked that before the death of Yeats, O'Connor began his disquisitions with 'As Yeats said to me'; after the death of his idol, he began 'As I said to Yeats'. The inevitable parting of the ways resulted in recrimination and bitterness.

Like many novelists and short-story writers, O'Connor's unaided efforts at playwriting were episodic and undisciplined. He was, despite his short-lived enthusiasm, not greatly interested in the theatre as an art-form. He had hoped to broaden the repertoire of the theatre by commissioning novelists, including himself, to write plays. His judgement of plays was erratic and he was accustomed to take a stand on behalf of plays which everybody else disliked. On the other hand, he dismissed as negligible the successful comedies of a good theatre craftsman like Louis D'Alton, who had learned his business as a journeyman actor-playwright in the hard world of the fit-ups.

[1] Frank O'Connor, *My Father's Son*, 1968, pp. 159–60.

By the late 1930s Dublin had shown that it was sufficiently mature to accept satire of national institutions in the plays of Paul Vincent Carroll and Denis Johnston. Some critics have contended that O'Casey's early plays had done much to heal the bitterness of the Civil War. O'Casey like Carroll and Johnston, seemed to say that patriotism was not enough. It was a natural reaction to the idealism of the fight for freedom which was now somewhat dulled by the stern realities of the everyday struggle for existence in a new and undeveloped state. A harsh literary censorship, although it did not apply to the stage, created a climate of repression which was not conducive to the free expression of ideas. Although playwrights remained uncommitted to any particular political ideology, the prevailing note was one of cynicism and disillusion. Yeats who had been a Senator in the Irish Free State Government, was still a father figure. In the early thirties, he began to flirt with a crypto-fascist movement, the Blueshirts. When he wished to stage *Coriolanus* in modern dress as a parable for the times, his fellow-directors opted for more conventional costuming. After Yeats's death, Ireland's neutrality in the Second World War made Irish drama of the period not only neutral but indifferent. This same indifference can be more deadly than the puritanism which usually precedes it. The later plays of Sean O'Casey such as *Cock-a-Doodle-Dandy* and *The Bishop's Bonfire*, in which he castigates an Ireland of his own imaginings, were nonchalantly dismissed as an old man's petulant joke. There were fewer protests and no riots in Dublin theatres. Apart from the customary internal dissension at the Abbey, there was no public controversy on the grand scale. It had been supplanted by a niggling negative criticism. Overseas, the Irish Theatre had gained status and prestige in the academic world. American tours by the Abbey in 1931 and 1938 found the children of those who had booed *The Playboy of the Western World* highly appreciative and obviously proud of the contributions of Ireland to world theatre. But there were ominous signs of a decline of standards at home. A poet and a university lecturer stood up in the Abbey stalls one night during a production of

The Plough and the Stars to protest not against the play but against the standards of production and acting. It is noteworthy that the O'Casey play was no longer a political issue but an accepted classic in which the performers might expect the vociferous criticism which Italians direct at opera singers. The idea was prevalent in Dublin that the Abbey, like Christmas, was not what it used to be. But as Lennox Robinson succinctly replied—it never was!

During and after the Second World War, the National Theatre produced several notable plays by M. J. Molloy, Bryan MacMahon, Louis D'Alton and Walter Macken, but, while no masterpieces emerged, things were not going at all badly up to the time of the disastrous Abbey fire in 1951. Now the Abbey seemed to have met the fate that the sourest of its critics had foretold for it; it seemed to have expired beneath a mountain of rubble and black ashes.

The fifteen years the company spent at the Queen's Theatre were in the nature of a Babylonian captivity. At times, it seemed that the work of half a century had gone for nothing. Some good work was done under difficulties. Walter Macken's *Home is the Hero* fulfilled the promise that he had shown in his earlier play, *Mungo's Mansion*. Louis D'Alton's satirical *This Other Eden* was a clever up-dating of the Irish question through an Englishman's eyes which was the subject of *John Bull's Other Island* nearly half a century earlier. Richard Johnston's *The Evidence I shall Give*, John Murphy's *The Country Boy* and Joseph Tomelty's *Is The Priest at Home* were of as high a standard as most of the plays which kept the theatre going in earlier decades. John McCann's comedies, *Give Me a Bed of Roses* and *I Know Where I'm Going*, although making greater concessions to popular appeal than was customary in the past, helped to lessen the financial burden which had arisen from the transfer to the Queen's.

M. J. Molloy, a Galway writer, who was closer in spirit to Synge and Colum than most of his contemporaries, was particularly successful in his dramatic reconstructions of a vanished Ireland in *The King of Friday's Men*, *The Paddy Pedlar* and *The Wood of the Whispering*. The dominant lyrical note gives his best work an authenticity which wins him a place with the folk-dramatists of the earlier period.

Many of the dramatists of the 1950s were closely connected with the thriving amateur movement which was a social and artistic phenomenon of the post-war years in rural Ireland. The links between amateur and professional activity were closer in Ireland than in countries where there had been an unbroken tradition of native drama.

With the decline of the great houses, amateur activity was centred around the garrison theatres where the military staged entertainments in drill-halls or in the mess. With the rise of artisan societies and working-men's clubs in the latter half of the nineteenth century, the popular melodramas of Boucicault were frequently staged by local groups in country towns. Occasionally, the more talented amateurs acted as walk-ons or played bit-parts with professional touring companies.

After the Abbey plays became widely known in rural Ireland, a new and indigenous amateur movement took shape where many of Ireland's best professionals got their first experience of the stage. With the spread of competitive amateur festivals in the late 1930s, hundreds of groups engaged in dramatic activities, in the winter months, in places where no touring company had ever ventured. An Amateur Drama Association of Ireland had been formed in 1932 with a view to developing the rôle of the amateur festivals. But it was not until the Amateur Drama Council of Ireland took control, in 1953, that the work proceeded on a country-wide basis. Hundreds of groups compete at their local festivals from which the winners go forward to the national finals in Athlone. The quality, of course, varies considerably from year to year and from place to place, but the general standard has been commendably high. Many groups make up for their lack of technique and professional polish by that intuitive drama sense which has been a characteristic of Irish theatre. Audiences who in the past were largely uncritical, as one would expect in the many parts of the country which are isolated from professional theatre, are nowadays more exacting. Moreover, the choice of plays is ambitious. Apart from the first productions of plays by such established playwrights as M. J. Molloy, Bryan MacMahon and Joseph Tomelty, the amateur movement can boast of its own discovery of the most popular playwright of the past two decades, John B. Keane.

In the annals of amateur drama, 1959 will be remembered as the year in which the Listowel Drama Group's production of *Sive* not only won the national award but set a local playwright, John B. Keane, on his way to becoming one of the most successful Irish playwrights of his generation. A great deal of the success of *Sive* was due to the Listowel Drama Group's outstanding presentation of this first play by a local playwright. They set a target for the best amateur groups who can fulfil a most important function by giving a platform to new plays of quality instead of producing the well-tried successes of the commercial theatres. In recent years, perhaps because of strong competition from television, the movement seems to have lost something of its former *élan*. It certainly has unearthed new talent in the acting field; but its theatre workshop rôle, with playwrights like M. J. Molloy, Bryan MacMahon or John B. Keane, working in unison with local producers and players, seems to have suffered an eclipse.

Much as John B. Keane is indebted to the amateur movement, they owe even more to him. The Southern Theatre Group, which was founded in Cork, on a semi-professional basis, has reaped a rich harvest from *Sive* and other Keane plays. This has enabled this Cork company to stage seasons of plays in commercial theatres in Cork, Limerick and, occasionally, in Dublin.

John B. Keane has wedded much of T. C. Murray's strength to the folk idiom of George Fitzmaurice, and the overall effect is eminently theatrical. If some of his plots are mechanical and contrived, he has the power to wring poetry out of the commonplace. Despite such obvious flaws as the weak scene-endings and the contrived letter scene, *Sive* generates an excitement in the theatre which withstands critical analysis. This is particularly true of the scenes in which the two tinkers with their 'bodhráns' and cursing-songs leave the audience breathless with excitement as if they had partaken in some primitive ritual. His best play, *The Field*, with a theme similar to *The Rugged Path*, is more theatrically effective today than George Shiels's popular success of the 1940s. Keane's picture of the greed, frustration and violence which grows from land-hunger would be practically unbearable were it not for the rich authentic dialogue and the salty humour with which the author can invest a tragic situation. *The Man from Clare* and *Hut 42*, both produced at the Abbey, have fine moments but they lack the cohesion and structural unity of *The Field*. Most of Keane's plays have at least one significant character, for example, 'Big Maggie', and one or two strong situations but they lack the essential unity of construction and theme so necessary for the two-hour traffic of the stage.

Closely allied to the amateur movement, the staging of plays in Irish has had a fitful career of starts and stops without ever getting really into its stride. The productions of Hyde's *Casadh an tSugáin* and Behan's *An Giall*, the original version of *The Hostage* are now part of theatre history. In the early years, the first productions of plays in Irish was in the hands of the Gaelic League. Later, groups such as Na hAisteóirí and An Comhar Drámaíochta did some interesting work in Dublin. None of these groups had a theatre of its own, moving from Edward Martyn's theatre to the Abbey, and later to the Peacock and the Gate. Although the groups had the occasional assistance of professional producers and players, the work was mainly in the hands of enthusiastic amateurs. Audiences were often more interested in the progress of the language or indeed in learning the language than in theatregoing as such. Such conditions were not propitious for the rise of a creative school of dramatists. There was a marked tendency to concentrate on translations or imitations of French farce and out-dated melodrama. The only permanent theatre for plays in Irish was in Galway where Micheál MacLiammóir's play *Diarmuid and Gráinne* was staged in 1928. Since then, An Taibhdhearc, as the Galway theatre is named, has survived with the benefit of a state grant. It has been more successful as a training-ground for players and producers such as Siobhán McKenna, Walter Macken, Frank Dermody and others, than as a source of original drama in Irish. In the 1950s and 1960s some interesting original plays were staged at the Damer Hall in Dublin under the auspices of Gael Linn. Although none of these became as well known as Behan's *An Giall*, playwrights such as Mairéad Ní Ghráda, Seán O Tuama, Criostóir O Floinn, Eoghan O Tuairisc and Diarmuid O Súilleabháin were given an opportunity to develop their talents. Some of the work of these playwrights has also been produced in the Peacock where the National Theatre stages plays in Irish as well as verse plays and some experimental work. Pantomimes and revues have also been staged in Irish at the Abbey and the Peacock. A small theatre has also been built in the Donegal Gaeltacht where plays are produced regularly. The fact remains that playwrights and players in Irish are still in search of an audience. If the Irish language had not continued to wilt as a spoken language, the National Theatre would be today mainly an Irish-speaking theatre. The language would have given a distinctive character not only to playwriting but to plays in translation.

In the early years, apart from four productions in Irish, the work of the Abbey was in English only. In 1912, Lady Gregory brought a native Irish speaker from Galway into the company to assist in the staging of a play in Irish. It was not until 1938 that a new effort was made by Ernest Blythe to recruit a company, the majority of whose members could play both in Irish and in English. Before the opening of the new Peacock, many short plays in Irish were staged after productions in English. Nowadays, although attendances do not always justify the effort, both full-length plays and one-acters are staged each season. This is not a new policy but a development of the ideas of the founders of the theatre. None the less, this bilingual approach has provoked some criticism not only from sections of the public who are unsympathetic to the language revival but from language supporters who feel that, even with a bilingual company, the productions in English will be the primary consideration. The Irish language still hovers between life and death; but it has been the inspiration of a great deal in the Irish theatre's past. That debt may one day be repaid.

CHAPTER ELEVEN

Rebels Without Riots

In 1950, a group organised by a quasi-religious society, Maria Duce, demonstrated against Seamus Byrne's IRA play, *Design for a Headstone*. The hecklers were neither as voluble nor as sincere as those who attacked *The Plough and the Stars*. The author was accused of being anti-this section of the IRA and anti-that section of the IRA and, to crown it all, 'agin the priests', which, of course, no IRA man or politician ever was! Particular exception was taken to a remark of a left-wing physical force character who quotes Voltaire's wish to see the last king being strangled with the gut of the last priest. All this must seem most bewildering to the serious playgoer elsewhere and those timid souls who invariably take to their heels when conflict literally spills over the footlights into the auditorium.

The author, on the other hand, may have been at fault in trying to portray so many diverse types of revolutionary that he succeeded in treading on too many corns at once. In the absence of any one central character around whom the storm of argument could swell, the exposition took on some of the characteristics of the left-wing scene itself—violent, muddle-headed and inconclusive.

The play was praised by some critics for the originality of its portrayal of prison life, and for exploring the dramatic possibilities of a hunger-strike. It seems to have been forgotten that Yeats, in *The King's Threshold*, had written of hunger-strike as a political weapon and revised the ending of his play after Terence McSwiney's heroic gesture in Brixton prison. Moreover, if the prison in Byrne's play is intended to be Mountjoy, there is a more authentic ring in Brendan Behan's *The Quare Fellow* with its 'old triangle that went jingle jangle along the banks of the Royal Canal'. Both IRA men at different points of their careers, it is interesting to compare Behan's dramatic treatment of the IRA in *The Hostage* with Byrne's in *Design for a Headstone*. Byrne's Conor Egan is on hunger-strike as a protest against a refusal of political treatment. The prison chaplain condemns Egan's hunger-strike, refuses him absolution and breaks his resolve before he dies from starvation. Egan is a veteran of the War of Independence and represents the link between the old IRA and the new IRA of the 1930s. He is the death-or-glory type, a die-hard of the Civil War and a Catholic who does not accept his bishop's pronouncements. Here is a recognisable and significant character. But it seems a pity that he is provided with a wife who only echoes O'Casey's Nora Clitheroe in showing the incompatibility of marriage and revolution from the woman's point of view. Some wives of revolutionaries welcomed the holocaust and roared and ranted like furies at every street corner.

Egan's deputy, Aidan O'Leary, represents an even more well-defined IRA point of view—that it is not only possible but imperative to be a fanatically 'good Catholic' and, at the same time, an unrelenting anti-cleric, as far as Maynooth politics of the 1922 period are concerned. He believes in a purely Irish culture and an uncompromising national outlook. He defends hunger-strikes and the execution of spies and informers. In his egotistic idealism, he is so well drawn that we recognise him immediately; indeed, he may be said to represent the popular idea of what an IRA man was and still is.

'Ructions' McGowan is a still more forceful creation with his quotations from Voltaire and Marx; he is in the left-wing tradition with Tone, Lalor, Connolly and Mellowes. A physical force man, he is a hater of what he believes to be the sham trappings of nationality: green-tape, the abracadabra of Army procedure, Finn McCool idolatry, the phrase-a-day attitude to the Irish language, and a masochistic cult of hunger-sacrifices and wrap-the-green-flag-round-me funerals. In the third act, his rebellion against the cold-blooded efficiency, or inefficiency, of the IRA's orders for the execution of a friendly warder, as a suspect spy, leads to an even more inefficient jail-break in which he loses his life. There are many supporting characters including the somewhat unconvincing prison chaplain, Father Maguire; but our interest is mainly centred on the uppermost frieze of revolutionaries, Egan, O'Leary and McGowan. It is a sincere and compelling portrayal and criticism of Irish revolutionary ideas and methods. But when one compares it with Behan's *The Hostage*, a more inchoate piece structurally, it remains clear that, in the theatre as in life, sincerity is not enough.

The thesis writers of the future will have a field-day when they come to examine the original drafts of Brendan Behan's *The Hostage*. First written in Irish, it was presented by Gael Linn under the title *An Giall* at the Damer Hall, St. Stephen's Green. The production was directed by Frank Dermody of the Abbey Theatre. The original Irish script, which had neither topical songs nor queers, underwent a sea-change on its transference across the Irish channel for its production in English at Joan Littlewood's Theatre Royal, Stratford East, London, in 1958. Indeed, one draft of the translation read as if it had been written on the mail-boat. The political allusions not only to Irish but international affairs, in the songs and dialogue, have been up-dated frequently for productions on both sides of the Atlantic. On a first reading the old IRA and the new, in *The Hostage*, are less credible and fully rounded characters than Seamus Byrne's revolutionaries. In this play, Behan does not portray the IRA in jail but in a brothel, where they are just part of an underground of prostitutes, homosexuals and do-gooders. An illegal army is seen as being on an equal footing with illegal sex. Despite the frequent revisions and the apparent inconsistencies, the basic situation remains the same in the Irish and English texts: a young English soldier is held as a hostage, in a Dublin brothel, for a young IRA prisoner who is to be hanged in a Belfast prison. The hostage falls in love with an Irish girl who is a servant in the brothel, but death ends the affair of the young lovers. In the version in Irish, the lyrical mood is more sustained and the political overtones do not dominate. In the Littlewood version, the canvas seems to sag at times under the repeated layers of comic varnish. But the text gives little indication of the theatrical excitement which this rollicking free-for-all engenders.

Despite its relevance to Irish revolutionary methods and to recent happenings in Northern Ireland, it would be wrong to overemphasise the political background of *The Hostage*. It is unlikely that Behan ever intended the English version as an authentic portrayal of the Irish political underground. This mocking and ribald send-up of the larger lunacies and quasi-religious fanaticism which, in this case, claim one innocent victim, has a wider significance even when measured against greater atrocities in Vietnam, Africa and the Middle East.

The blend of music-hall knockabout with compassion and magnanimity, has enabled the play to cross many frontiers. A hostage lives and loves and dies to a madhouse chorus of bawdy bawls, craw-thumping hymns and randy laughter. Outside in the darkness, humanity weeps at the pity of it all. The hostage can only burst into song at the sheer futility of his end:

> The bells of hell
> Go ting-a-ling-a-ling
> For you but not for me
> Oh death where is thy
> Sting-a-ling-a-ling
> Or grave thy victory.

It is the dead soldier who has the last ironic word in a mad world:

> If you meet the undertaker,
> Or the young man from the Pru'...
> Get a pint with what's left over
> Now I'll say goodbye to you.

Within a framework as flexible as a variety show, Behan with mocking gallows humour makes a final and total protest against man's inhumanity to man. Critics have pointed out that the central situation of *The Hostage* bears a close resemblance to Frank O'Connor's brilliant IRA story, *Guests of the Nation*. But this story is based on an incident in Kerry during the war of Independence. The mood and treatment is entirely Behan's own with embellishments by Joan Littlewood and others. For Irish audiences, the most satisfying production was that directed by Hugh Hunt at the Abbey in 1970.

We are back again in the Mountjoy of *Design for a Headstone* in *The Quare Fellow*. The device of the running commentary to describe events off-stage is the only similarity. Politics, legal or illegal, do not concern Behan in this play. The first version was a one-act piece, *The Twisting of Another Rope*, which he submitted to the Abbey. He was asked to develop it as a full-length play. He did so to such an extent that it would require five hours playing time. The play was returned to him to shorten, but it was not resubmitted. After its production at the Pike in Dublin and at Joan Littlewood's Theatre Workshop in London, it was eventually staged at the Abbey in 1956.

The Quare Fellow is a more tightly constructed play than *The Hostage*. Yet, it remains a play without a central character. The condemned man who is known as *The Quare Fellow* never appears on stage. We see and hear the reactions of his fellow-prisoners and warders to his execution. There is no question of the punishment fitting the crime, no easy sentimentality about the condemned man never having a chance to go straight, no Sydney Carton heroics as the condemned man steps to the scaffold. The punishment is the crime. Gabriel Marcel, the distinguished French playwright and philosopher wrote of it in *Les Nouvelles Litteraires*:

There is nothing in it resembling an open indictment (of capital punishment) and it is precisely because of that that the play touches us so acutely. We see how human beings who, one way or another, participate in the execution of the sentence, react to it, and that reaction is itself a judgment.

Now that capital punishment is no longer a subject of major controversy in England and Ireland, *The Quare Fellow* has lost some of its original impact. But it is neither a problem play nor a documentary on judicial hanging. The scenes of prison life in which jailers and jailed face the grim daily round with sardonic acceptance have a theatrical vitality of their own which raises what might have been a mere thesis play to the level of tragicomedy.

It may well be that Frank McMahon's adaptation of Behan's autobiography *Borstal Boy* may be Behan's most enduring contribution to the theatre. First produced by Tomás MacAnna at the Abbey in 1967, three years after Behan's death, it has since been played in Paris and New York, where it won the Critics Award as the best Broadway play of 1970.

It is now over thirty years since Behan first began to write of his experiences as a Borstal Boy:

> I awoke on the morning of 7 February 1940, with a feeling of despondency. I'd had a restless night and fell asleep only to be awakened an hour later by the bell that aroused myself and 1,235 other prisoners in Walton Jail.

So begins a chronicle of jails which appeared under the title *I Became a Borstal Boy* in the June 1942 edition of the Irish magazine *The Bell*. Later he published excerpts in the Paris magazine *Points* and in other newspapers and periodicals. But the work was not completed in book form until 1958. Behan gave more time and thought to the composition of *Borstal Boy* than to any other of his works.

The autobiography has all the mocking gallows humour of *The Quare Fellow*, the devil-may-care exuberance of *The Hostage*, as well as the compassion and sensibility of his best short story, *The Confirmation Suit*. Here was something new in Irish writing—the jail journal of a teenager illumined by an indestructible innocence. Behan, a Borstal Boy by political mischance, takes hard knocks but he gives back all he got and more. He never moans or groans about what he suffered. Behind the fusillade of four-letter abuse, one can detect a liking for screws, coppers and Englishmen. Beneath the violence and the crudities, there is an irrepressible gaiety and the saving grace of mother wit. Although it was recognised internationally as a significant work, it was denied circulation in Australia and New Zealand, and banned for a period in the Republic of Ireland. It was too outrageously funny to appeal to doctrinaire republicans, too warmly human for those committed to left-wing dialectics. Bemused by this local comedy of errors, Behan tried to laugh off the whole affair with a parody of MacNamara's Band:

> My name is Brendan Behan
> I'm the best-banned in the land.

But when the literary and intellectual côteries in Dublin remained strangely silent about the ban on *Borstal Boy*, he suffered a deep hurt. It was sad that he did not live to see the Abbey stage version, which preserved most of the outstanding qualities of a book which, for twelve years, could not be obtained in his native city.

Three of Behan's pieces for radio, *Moving Out, A Garden Party* and *The Big House*, were staged at the Gate by Alan Simpson, under the general title, *The New House*. The first two are humorous inconsequential accounts based on the move of the Behan family from O'Casey country, in Russell Street, to a new housing estate in Crumlin. We meet the Behans, alias the Hannigans, living in a tenement when news comes that they have got a new Corporation house in distant Crumlin. The mother, in an effort to better her lot and that of her family, wastes no time in moving but the husband does not relish the idea of leaving his pals and his pubs for what he considers the wilds of the country. He returns home one evening to find a curt note that his tea would be served in what he regards as the concrete jungle of Ardee Road. Although he has been given a wrong number, he eventually finds the house. True to Behan's sense of fun and understanding, we find that though the location of the home was changed, the people haven't changed. To paraphrase the Roman philosopher: 'Men may change the sky above their heads but not the heart within the breast'; so the Hannigan family remain their own dear selves.

The companion piece, *A Garden Party*, deals in hilarious fashion with the suburban problems of digging the garden. The husband goes to preposterous extremes to avoid becoming a horny-handed tiller of the soil. *The Big House* is less sure-footed when Behan attempts to write dialogue for the Anglo-Irish gentry, a class he could joke about but could not write about. He was more at his ease, even in the unfinished fragment, *Richard's Cork Leg*, where he strings together all the leftovers from *The Hostage* and *The Quare Fellow*. Behan's dialogue owed nothing to O'Casey and only a little to Joyce. But these minor pieces reveal a major weakness, one common among other Irish playwrights, a fatal fluency, an uncontrolled gift of the gab.

The Irish Government gave the Abbey an excellently designed and splendidly equipped modern theatre in 1966 on the old site. But there were critics who remained unconvinced. Some were of the opinion that giving such a theatre to the Abbey was akin to putting a Christian Dior creation on a barefooted Connemara colleen.

Since 1966, the company has visited Florence, Vienna, Brussels, Paris, Edinburgh, Frankfurt and London and had a large share in the success of Brendan Behan's *Borstal Boy* in New York and Toronto. Provincial tours in Ireland have been resumed after a lapse of a quarter of a century. For the first time ever, the Abbey has brought plays in Irish to the Aran Islands and the Irish-speaking districts in the West.

The spread of the amateur movement and the advent of television has made it difficult for the National Theatre to revive some of the popular Abbey successes of earlier years. The realistic comedies of life in country towns and the minor joys and sorrows of suburbia, which were the stock-in-trade of many Abbey dramatists, have either been produced on television or have been done to death by amateurs. Moreover, the work of many of the better Abbey realists are rooted in the past and no longer appear relevant in a changing Ireland.

Most of the best plays written in Ireland in the past quarter-century, whether staged at the Abbey or elsewhere, conform to the Abbey pattern. Although not all of the plays of M. J. Molloy, Walter Macken, John B. Keane, Brendan Behan, Brian Friel, Eugene McCabe and Thomas Murphy are set in kitchens, tenements or prisons, they are all written within a naturalistic framework but make use of somewhat non-naturalistic dialogue, often with poetic overtones. It was O'Casey who took the Abbey play into the tenement just as Brendan Behan took it behind prison walls and into the brothel. Brian Friel, who is technically the most accomplished of living Irish playwrights, shows us the country boy setting off for America in *Philadelphia Here I Come* and shows us the Irish countrywoman coming home from the States in *The Loves of Cass Maguire*. His first Abbey play, *The Enemy Within*, depicts a monastic settlement in early Christian times on the Island of Iona. It is a warm, human play with the kind of clerical characters one meets in the early stories of Frank O'Connor; but, although the principal character, Saint Colmcille, was a prince of royal blood, he is surrounded by peasants in cassocks. The technique may have changed, but the gift for dialogue is the constant factor in all of Friel's plays and in the best work of his contemporaries. Without this gift for dialogue, any Brendan Behan play would be a mere shambles.

This concentration on racy dialogue in a rural or tenement setting is understandable in a country where most town and country dwellers, rich and poor, Catholic and Protestant, are relatively unsophisticated and only one or two removes from the land. Most Irish playwrights have either accepted this fact or depicted their characters as reacting to it, like the rather pompous Canon in *Shadow and Substance* who spends a great deal of his time bemoaning the vulgarity of his niece who links him by law to a cattle-jobber, or reprimanding his curates for their behaviour as frocked farmers. Behan reacts in a similar manner with his swipes at 'Bogmen' and 'Culchies', epithets usually reserved by the city-bred for anybody born further west than the Phoenix Park.

Of course, colourful dialogue, quaint expressions and 'poetry-talk' are not confined to plays. This is also evident in many short stories and novels by Irish writers. In recent years, good theatre craftsmen have prepared stage adaptations of well-known stories and novels. P. J. O'Connor's adaptations of *The Tailor and Ansty* and Patrick Kavanagh's semi-autobiographical *Tarry Flynn*, as staged at the Abbey captured the quality of the originals. The best known internationally are Frank MacMahon's adaptation of Behan's *The Borstal Boy* and Hugh Leonard's *Stephen D*, an adaptation of James Joyce's *A Portrait of the Artist as a Young Man* and *Stephen Hero*.

The original Dublin Theatre Festival production by Jim Fitzgerald was perhaps the most spell-binding piece of stage-craft seen in Dublin since Hilton Edwards's presentation of *The Skin of our Teeth* by Thornton Wilder. This heady brew not only induced an uncritical euphoria among theatregoers who professed to know their Joyce but completely floored some American critics who seem to have confused him with the author of *English as We Speak It in Ireland*—a book by Joyce (Patrick Weston) which some Irishmen have always preferred to anything written by Joyce (James Augustine).

Nobody who saw that first production is likely to forget those early scenes where Stephen Dedalus (Norman Rodway) like an ineffectual fallen angel stood guard at the gate of lost innocence. Not less memorable was the *frisson* which tingled through the auditorium as the late Gerard Healy delivered the Hell Sermon in tones like rapiers of ice.

Much of *Stephen D* was magnificent, but it was not Joyce. Hugh Leonard not only stacked the cards expertly and covertly in his own favour, but he played out of two packs at the same time. The danger with this procedure is that the dealer—in this case, the adaptor—ends up not with four aces but with five. The extra ace had been culled from a rejected pack, the rough draft of *A Portrait of the Artist as a Young Man*, which was posthumously published under the title *Stephen Hero*. The temptation to transpose from the rejected earlier version must have been irresistible to an accomplished theatre craftsman. *Stephen Hero* is not only a more explicit and less introvert exposition of a troubled and tormented adolescence but its straightforward episodic manner makes it more tractable material for stage presentation. In the *Portrait*, the action is more fluid; scenes of childhood and adolescence shuttle backward and forward with a more subtle emphasis. While much of *Stephen Hero* is rudimentary and crude, the *Portrait* is a consummate and universal work of art. It is hardly surprising that *Stephen D*, in which portions of a rough pencil sketch are pinned to the flawless canvas of the *Portrait* has some of the eccentricity and idiosyncrasy of a collage.

The stage version over-emphasises puberty, irreverence and revolt for revolt's sake. Stephen Dedalus's rejection of home, faith and fatherland is powerfully portrayed but there is scarcely a suggestion of the purpose of this renunciation. Neither Stephen nor Joyce was driven into exile. In both cases, the exile was voluntary and it was prompted by a sincere creative and imaginative impulse: 'I go to encounter for the millionth time the reality of experience and to forge in the smithy of my soul the uncreated conscience of my race.' The chosen implements were 'silence, exile and cunning'.

One misses the fundamental Irishness of the *Portrait* where Joyce's youth in Dublin is crystallised. What was very Irish was the reaction to this expertly mounted piece of theatre which gave another opportunity to the mealy-mouthed to voice again their protests against the blasphemy and bawdy of Joyce, who, of course, was not a party to the affair, except in so far as he might have shown a little more of his cherished 'cunning' in the choice of literary executors.

Joyce, like Edward Martyn, was a fervid Ibsenite, and from his youth had rejected the idea of a native Irish drama. In his only play, *Exiles*, he is clearly indebted to his Norwegian master. It is set in Dublin but the mood is introspective and lacks any trace of the humour of his native city which he captured so faithfully in *Ulysses*. He seems cabined and confined in the dramatic form. He cannot stride the streets of Dublin which, in his prose works, echo with his gigantic cosmic laughter. He steered clear of the Irish dramatic movement as a snare, unable to accept Yeats's principle of a return to the people as a basis for art. He and Martyn denied that any people or society can be fully interpreted in so arbitrary a manner. Another distinguished Irish expatriate of today, Samuel Beckett, would hardly accept the Yeatsian principle either.

It is widely believed in Dublin that Beckett once acted as Joyce's secretary and that the influence of one Dubliner on another, especially of a famous one on an unknown, is as obvious as it is irresistible. The truth of the matter is that Beckett, like others of Joyce's friends in Paris, occasionally read to and took dictation from an almost blind man. Their Dublin backgrounds were totally dissimilar—Joyce's middle-class shabby genteel, Catholic; Beckett's well-to-do, respectable, Protestant. Beckett, except for occasional visits for family funerals, has distanced himself completely from the city of his birth. Joyce's physical exile from Dublin was more total but, on the psychic plane, he never left it. The Irish references in Beckett's plays are tentative, tangential, and remain on the periphery of his no-man's never-never land. Joyce, like Stephen Dedalus, strode into eternity along Sandymount Strand.

Waiting for Godot, staged in Dublin at the Pike Theatre, is now widely accepted as the most original contribution to dramatic literature since the Second World War. Those who like theatrical labels arbitrarily list its author, Samuel Beckett, as a forerunner of the Theatre of the Absurd. The label generalizes unfairly. But it may serve a purpose in so far as the playgoer who comes to a Beckett play with preconceived ideas, will be jolted into acceptance of a new form. In the case of *Waiting for Godot*, there will be nearly as many interpretations as there are people in the audience. The two tramps Didi and Gogo, for short, will mentally rub shoulders with Weary Willie and Tired Tim of the comic strips, with Shem and Shaun of *Finnegans Wake*, with Itch and Scratch, the two lousy comedians of the Music Hall, and with the two hobos, in Lord Dunsany's play,

The Glittering Gate, who uncork an infinity of empty beer bottles in a heaven that is nothing but 'bloomin' great stars'.

Such facile identifications are finally fruitless because *Waiting for Godot* is a play which all the time is trying to avoid definition. In a play by Balzac, a mysterious character named Godeau arrives with money to solve everybody's problems. That Beckett's Godot does not come is what makes the play a parable of life as seen by modern man. Beckett is not a forerunner or a practitioner of the Theatre of the Absurd, but he is the first playwright of the Space Age. A dramatic astronaut, he views life on earth with a wry sadness through vistas of space. In his later plays, the characters do not communicate in the ordinary sense—but as if through the unsatisfactory and repetitive medium of the talk-back of a translunar communications system. One of his plays, *Breath*, with a playing time of thirty seconds, has no characters at all. One senses that he would gladly be rid of the actor completely and present his plays with computerised automatons emitting sounds in Basic French or Basic English from multi-track tapes. His ideal medium is perhaps radio in which the *vox humana* can now be produced electronically in impersonal grunts and groans.

It has often been noted that when Irish plays are staged in London or New York, they seem to suffer a sea-change when Irish actors are not employed. Synge, O'Casey and, to a lesser extent, Behan and Brian Friel have suffered in this respect. The very authenticity of the dialogue, its rhythm and poetic imagery, demand interpreters who are reasonably familiar with Irish usage. It is in this respect that an 'outsider' like Beckett, writing first in French and later translating into English, with faint undertones of Dublin middle-class usage, has a distinct advantage as far as the interpretation of his works on the international stage is concerned.

It was Roger Blin who first launched that Gallic-Gaelic sputnik, *En Attendant Godot* at the Theatre de Babylone, Paris, in 1953. Since then it has been translated into at least fifteen languages and played in twenty countries. The Abbey staged it, somewhat belatedly, in 1969, to honour the third Dubliner to win the Nobel Prize for Literature. A few years earlier, the first productions in English of his *Come and Go* and *Play* were presented in the Peacock. But the Abbey's closest link with Beckett is that a former Abbey actor, the late Jack McGowran, became his finest interpreter.

The recent dependence of the Irish theatre on adaptations has been noted. A great deal of dramatic work since the days of the Greeks has been derivative as far as the basic material is concerned. But a dearth of original creative work would certainly pose problems for a National Theatre. Since the Abbey was founded, it has staged over five hundred new plays by Irish authors or on Irish subjects. Although a considerable number of these barely reached the border-line of acceptability, the theatre has continued to provide an outlet for Irish talent and, on occasions, genius. There have been periods when in the absence of worthwhile original plays, plays translated from Continental languages and plays over one hundred years old have been staged not only to compensate for the dearth of original work but to make audiences and playwrights aware of trends in international drama. This also gave the company experience in different fields of dramatic endeavour. Plays of international repute such as Brecht's *Galileo*, Genet's *The Maids*, Lorca's *Yerma* and Gunther Grass's *The Plebians Rehearse the Uprising* avoid the pitfalls of a narrow insularity and are clearly compatible with the work for which the theatre was founded. Much experimental work takes place in the Abbey's sister theatre, the Peacock. The future of the Irish theatre, may well rest in a development of the Peacock's rôle as a theatre workshop where young playwrights, young actors and young audiences can shape the drama of tomorrow.

Another notable trend is a growing interest in documentary theatre. The Dublin Theatre Festival in 1971 presented Conor Cruise O'Brien's *Murderous Angels* in which he portrays his experiences as an United Nations Official in the Congo somewhat in the manner of *Vietnam Discours* by Peter Weiss and Hochhuth's *Soldiers*. Such essays in the Theatre of Fact are frequently assailed on the grounds that the facts prove to be fictions; but they are indicative of an attempt to make theatre relevant to world politics and problems.

Many are of the view that the Irish theatre must now strive to break from the rut of tradition in which it has become embedded. The plays and players which made the theatre famous were a new phenomenon on the theatrical scene. The playwrights and players of today are the inheritors and part upholders of that tradition. It should be an easier and perhaps no less rewarding task to break from the tradition than to create it. Much as some playwrights may resent the fact, the theatre calls for a high degree of collaboration between producer, actor and author if the final product is to succeed before an audience. Plots and themes whether taken from history, legend or fiction and adapted for the stage, stand or fall ultimately on how they are handled in terms of theatre. Everybody who works in the theatre must, to coin a phrase, woo an audience somewhere or somehow. On the opening night of the old Abbey Theatre, Yeats made an uncharacteristic speech which is seldom quoted: 'Authors must be free to choose their own way but in their pilgrimage towards beauty and truth they require companions by the way.'[1] The companions he had in mind were an audience large enough to fill the new Abbey and Peacock theatres.

If dramatic writing appears to be in a blind alley, this is a challenge to the playwrights of the future to make a brave leap in the dark. Everywhere there seems to be a decay of invention and a dearth of good original material. New tensions in Irish life demand new treatments in dramatic form. If the Irish writer is going to respond to the changing scene in life and in the theatre, he will have to break new ground. There will still be a place for the play written in the traditional style. Perhaps due to an overlong period of picture and proscenium stages and an overlong reign of a set of conventions which are conveniently labelled realistic, the fundamentals may have been overlooked. In this age of television, the theatre should be unashamedly theatrical and it should exploit its distinct advantage over both cinema and television in accepting unreservedly that the play-

Lennox Robinson, *Ireland's Abbey Theatre, A History*, 1951, p. 47.

wright, actor and audience—are interdependent and complementary. A play can only be judged in performance. Whether Greek tragedy or kitchen comedy, it cannot be assessed by reading the script or from a summary of the plot by a critic. The physical immediacy of the stage presence, an actor playing to an audience and reacting to an audience, this is the prerequisite for judgement. It is this readiness of the public to assess plays in performance, in their visual and aural elements, that has kept the Irish theatre alive. The audience looks forward with expectancy to each new play in the hope that it will provide, at least, the scaffolding for the drama of the future. As this chapter is being written, a highly original Abbey play, *The Morning After Optimism*, by Thomas Murphy, has pricked the bubbles of illusion and scattered some of the shadow-dreams of the past. It is too early to claim that Irish playwriting has entered a new supranational phase. But there are signs that audiences are no longer satisfied with the inbreedings of the past. There are still some who foolishly expect a steady succession of masterpieces. But the spirit bloweth where it listeth. Others, deeply conscious of the movement's vital and tempestuous past, lament a present decline. It may not be the Irish Theatre which they lament but their own lost youth and a fading capacity for enjoyment of what the playwrights and players can still offer.

Bibliography

General Works

Boyd, Ernest A.: *Ireland's Literary Renaissance*, Dublin and London, 1916.
  A comprehensive account of the literary revival including the dramatic movement between 1880 and 1916.

Clark, William Smith: *The Early Irish Stage*, Oxford at the Clarendon Press, 1955.
  A well-documented account of the initial period of Dublin Theatre.

Duggan, G. C.: *The Stage Irishman: A History of the Irish Play and Stage Characters from the Earliest Times*, Dublin, 1937.
  Particularly useful for its comments on plays on Irish subjects and on the evolution of the stage Irishman.

Fay, Gerard: *The Abbey Theatre*, Dublin, 1958.
  Particularly useful for its evaluation of the work of the Fay Brothers in the foundation of the National Theatre.

Gregory, Lady: *Our Irish Theatre*, London, 1914.
  An intimate account of the beginnings of the modern Irish drama and of the early days of the Abbey.

Hogan, Robert: *After the Irish Renaissance. A Critical History of the Irish Drama since the Plough and the Stars*, Minneapolis, 1967.
  A comprehensive account of the work of Irish playwrights since 1926. Particularly useful for references to interesting but relatively obscure plays staged in Dublin and elsewhere.

Hobson, Bulmer (Editor): *The Gate Theatre—Dublin*, Dublin 1934.
  A short illustrated record of the achievements of the Dublin Gate Theatre with a list and dates of productions between 1928 and 1934.

BIBLIOGRAPHY

Malone, Andrew E.: *The Irish Drama*, London, 1914.
A comprehensive survey of the achievements of the Irish Theatre from 1899 to 1928.
Robinson, Lennox (Compiler): *Ireland's Abbey Theatre. A History, 1899–1951*, London, 1951.
An official history which includes the dates and complete casts of all productions of the Irish Literary Theatre and its successor the Abbey Theatre.

Historical, Biographical and Critical Works

Bentley, Eric: *In Search of Theatre*, London, 1954.
Bickley, Francis: *J. M. Synge and the Irish Dramatic Movement*, London, 1912.
Blythe, Ernest: *The Abbey Theatre*, Dublin (n.d.).
Bourgeois, Maurice, *John Millington Synge and the Irish Theatre*, London, 1913.
Boyd, Ernest A.: *Contemporary Drama of Ireland*, Dublin, 1917.
Byrne, Dawson: *Ireland's National Theatre*, Dublin, 1929.
Chetwood, William Rufus: *The British Theatre: Containing the Lives of the English Dramatic Poets . . . With the Lives of Most of the Principal Actors*, London, 1752.
Clark, Barrett: *A Study of Modern Drama*, New York, 1926.
Cole, Toby and Chinoy, Helen Krich: *Actors on Acting: The Theories and Techniques, and Practices of the Great Actors of All Times*, New York, 1949–54.
Coquelin, Constant, Henry Irving and Dion Boucicault: *The Art of Acting*. Published for the Dramatic Museum of Columbia University, 1926.
Corkery, Daniel: *Synge and Anglo-Irish Literature*, Cork, 1931.
Cowasjee, Saros: *Sean O'Casey: The Man Behind the Plays*, Edinburgh, 1963.
Coxhead, Elizabeth: *Lady Gregory*, London, 1961.
Edwards, Hilton: *The Mantle of Harlequin*, Dublin, 1958.
Ellis-Fermor, Una: *The Irish Dramatic Movement*, London, 1939.
Ervine, St. J. G.: *Some Impressions of My Elders*, London, 1922.
Ervine, St. J. G.: *The Theatre in My Time*, London, 1933.
Fallon, Gabriel: *The Abbey and the Actor*, Dublin, 1969.
Fallon, Gabriel: *Sean O'Casey, The Man I Knew*, London, 1965.

Fay, W. G. and Carswell, Catherine: *The Fays of the Abbey Theatre*, London, 1935.
Flannery, James W.: *Miss Annie F. Horniman and the Abbey Theatre*, Dublin, 1970.
Gelb, Arthur and Gelb, Barbara: *O'Neill*, London, 1962.
Greene, David J. and Stephens, Edward M.: *J. M. Synge*, New York, 1959.
Gregory, Lady Augusta, *Lady Gregory's Journals*, ed. Lennox Robinson, London, 1946.
Gregory, Lady: *Our Irish Theatre*, London, 1914; New York, 1965.
Gwynn, Denis; *Edward Martyn and the Irish Revival*, London, 1930.
Gwynn, Stephen: *Irish Literature and Drama*, Dublin, 1937.
Hitchcock, Robert: *An Historical View of the English Stage*, 2 vols., Dublin, 1788-94.
Hogan, Robert: *Dion Boucicault*, New York, 1969.
Holloway, Joseph: *Joseph Holloway's Abbey Theatre*, eds. Robert Hogan and Michael J. O'Neill, Carbondale, 1967.
Hone, Joseph: *The Life of George Moore*, London, 1936.
Hone, Joseph: *W. B. Yeats. A Biography*, London, 1942.
Howe, P. P.: *J. M.-Synge*, London, 1912.
Hughes, Samuel C.: *The Pre-Victorian Drama of Dublin*, Dublin, 1904.
Hyde, Douglas: *Love Songs of Connacht*, Introduction by Micheal Ó hAodha, Shannon, Ireland, 1969.
James, Henry: *The Scenic Art. Notes on Acting and the Drama, 1872-1902*, London, 1949.
Kane, Whitford: *Are We All Met?* London, 1931.
Kavanagh, Peter: *The Irish Theatre*, Tralee, 1946.
Kavanagh, Peter: *The Story of the Abbey Theatre*, New York, 1950.
Keane, John B.: *Self Portrait*, Cork, 1964.
Kirkman, James Thomas: *Memoirs of the Life of Charles Macklin, Esq.*, 2 vols., London, 1799.
Koslow, Jules: *Sean O'Casey: the man and his plays*, New York, 1950.
Krause, David (Editor): *The Dolmen Press Boucicault*, Dublin, 1964.
Krause, David: *Sean O'Casey: The Man and His Work*, London, 1960.
MacLiammóir, Micheál: *All for Hecuba*, London, 1946.
MacLiammóir, Micheál: *Theatre in Ireland*, 2nd edn, Dublin, 1964.
MacLysaght, Edward: *Irish Life in the Seventeenth Century*, Cork and Oxford, 1950.
Margulies, Martin B.: *The Early Life of Seán O'Casey*, Dublin, 1970.
McCann, Seán (Editor): *The World of Seán O'Casey*, 1966.

BIBLIOGRAPHY

Mercier, Vivian: *The Irish Comic Tradition*, Oxford University Press, 1962.
Nicoll, Allardyce: *The English Theatre*, London, 1936.
Nic Shiubhlaigh, Máire: *The Splendid Years*, Dublin, 1955.
O'Connor, Frank: *The Art of the Theatre*, Dublin, 1947.
O'Connor, Frank: *My Father's Son* (Autobiography), Dublin, 1968.
O'Connor, Ulick: *Brendan Behan*, London, 1970.
O'Neill, Michael J.: *Lennox Robinson*, New York, 1964.
Pogson, Rae: *Miss Horniman and the Gaiety Theatre, Manchester*, London, 1952.
Robinson, Lennox (Editor): *The Irish Theatre*, London, 1939.
Robinson, Lennox: *Curtain Up*, London, 1942.
Simpson, Alan: *Beckett and Behan and a Theatre in Dublin*, London, 1962.
Stockwell, La Tourette: *Dublin Theatre and Theatre Customs (1637–1820)*, Kingsport, Tennessee, 1938.
Strong, L. A. G.: *John Millington Synge*, London, 1941.
Ure, Peter: *Yeats the Playwright*, London, 1963.
Walsh, Townsend: *The Career of Dion Boucicault*, New York, 1915.
Weygandt, Cornelius: *Irish Plays and Playwrights*, London, 1913.
Wilks, Robert: *Memoirs of the Life of Robert Wilks, Esq.*, London, 1732.
Yeats, W. B.: *Autobiographies*, London, 1955.
Yeats, W. B.: *Dramatis Personae*, London, 1936.
Yeats, W. B.: *Explorations*, London, 1962.
Yeats, W. B.: *Plays and Controversies*, London, 1923.